HIROSHIMA
AND
NAGASAKI
Retrospect and Prospect

Edited by
DOUGLAS HOLDSTOCK
and
FRANK BARNABY

FRANK CASS • LONDON

First published in Great Britain by
FRANK CASS & CO LTD
Newbury House, 900 Eastern Avenue
London EG2 7HH, England

and in the United States by
FRANK CASS
c/o ISBS
5804 N.E. Hassalo Street, Portland, Oregon 97213-3644

Copyright © 1995 Frank Cass & Co. Ltd.

Library of Congress Cataloging-in-Publication Data

Applied for.

British Library Cataloguing in Publication Data

Applied for.

ISBN 0-7146-4667-9 (hb)
ISBN 0-7146-420409 – Wrong ISBN

This group of studies first appeared in a Special Issue on 'Hiroshima and Nagasaki: Retrospect and Prospect' in *Medicine and War*, Vol.11, No.3, published by Frank Cass & Co. Ltd.

Typeset by Regent Typesetting, London.
Printed in Great Britain by Progressive Printing (UK) Limited, Leigh-on-Sea, Essex.

HIROSHIMA AND NAGASAKI

Contents

Foreword

I am become death, the destroyer of worlds

These words from the *Bhagavad Gita* came to the mind of Robert Oppenheimer, leader of the Manhattan Project, as he witnessed the first man-made nuclear explosion at Alamogordo, New Mexico, on 16 July 1945. Within the next few months death came indeed to some 200,000 inhabitants of the Japanese cities of Hiroshima and Nagasaki. The world has not been the same place since: humankind has the capacity to destroy its own civilization, perhaps to bring itself to the point of extinction, and to produce an ecological catastrophe unparalleled since a meteorite impact sixty million years ago brought about the demise of the dinosaurs.[1-3]

This publication looks back to what happened at Hiroshima, though perhaps less eloquently than has been done elsewhere,[4] why it happened, and where we stand fifty years later. We have 'muddled through' the intervening half-century,[5] and nuclear weapons stockpiles are for the first time being reduced. Even when existing treaties are fully implemented there will still be more than enough to cause a nuclear winter.[6] No more cities have been razed, though over 1900 tests have been carried out, the latest in May of this year (1995) by China, and it now appears that France is to carry out a further series. These tests had a total destructive yield 40,000 times that of the Hiroshima bomb, and 400,000 people may have died or will die from the effects of the fallout.[7]

We believe, though, that anniversaries are a time to look forward as well as back, and our contributors also look at today's world and share hopes and fears for the next fifty years. We have not tried to write a text-book about nuclear weapons or a history of the nuclear arms race, though some basic information is included, but have encouraged each individual to express his or her own views. This has led to some repetition, for which we do not apologise: all share the wish for a nuclear-weapon-free world, and none are denied the chance to say so.

It is a truism that prevention is better than cure, and, as was the case at Hiroshima and Nagasaki, there is no effective treatment for the victims of nuclear war. As Professor Victor Sidel describes, doctors have been in the forefront of efforts to prevent it, and one of the founders of the physicians' initiative, Australian paediatrician Dr Helen Caldicott, has called the abolition of nuclear weapons 'the ultimate form of preventive medicine'.[8] Dr Caldicott's work helped to inspire the founding of International Physicians for the Prevention of Nuclear War, of which Professor Sidel is now Co-President. Mikhail Gorbachev has acknowledged the influence of the physicians' movement on his own thinking and hence the end of the Cold War.[9]

Kazuyo Yamane shows that peace overtures were coming from Japan well before the bombs were dropped, with the obvious implication that they were a warning to the Soviet Union as well as a weapon of the Second World War. Paul Rogers warns that, as the risk of East–West confrontation fades, nuclear weapons will become a threat across a widening North–South divide, and Jasjit Singh fears that fissile materials or even warheads, particularly from the former Soviet Union, could end up in the hands of unscrupulous governments or even terrorist groups. The recent gas attack on the Tokyo underground and the Oklahoma City outrage show just how ruthless such groups have become, and the threat of a terrorist nuclear attack would cause total panic.

We believe that there is an indissoluble link between nuclear weapons and civil nuclear power. The first nuclear reactors were built to make plutonium for nuclear weapons (the Nagasaki bomb used plutonium as fissile material, as do the majority of today's nuclear warheads), and only as an afterthought was it realized that the heat produced in reactors could be used to generate electricity. Of the non-nuclear weapon states, Japan is the most reliant on nuclear power for its energy needs, and Shaun Burnie describes the large accumulation of plutonium that it has acquired and will inevitably continue to acquire if present policies continue. Much of this is in a form immediately available for bomb-making, and with its expertise in electronics Japan could have nuclear weapons capability within weeks. This is in a region where China is an established nuclear weapon state and North Korea is under suspicion of wanting nuclear weapons – both traditional rivals of Japan. Its reliance on nuclear power and political links (but also increasing commercial rivalry) with the United States may, suggests Kazuyo Yamane, be leading to an ambiguous attitude to nuclear weapons in Japan as memories of Hiroshima and Nagasaki become more distant.

While nuclear weapons are instruments of national politics, opposition to them has been from dedicated individuals, usually at grassroots level. We have already mentioned Dr Helen Caldicott, and the Greenham Common Women's Peace Camps have a place in history. As Robert Green describes, the World Court Project began around a kitchen table in New Zealand, yet it has persuaded the World Health Organization and the United Nations General Assembly to question the legality of nuclear weapons before the world's premier legal body, the International Court of Justice at The Hague.

We should like to take this opportunity to pay a special tribute to our most distinguished contributor, Joseph Rotblat. He worked on the Manhattan Project when it was feared that Germany, through distinguished physicists such as Werner Heisenberg, would make a nuclear bomb, but left the project when it became clear that this would not happen.

Throughout a long life, he has worked tirelessly, mainly through the Pugwash movement, to rid the world of nuclear weapons. His chapter comes almost at the end only because a nuclear-weapon-free world is the final goal: no one has worked harder to achieve this. As Rotblat concludes, the need for such a world is the ultimate lesson of Hiroshima and Nagasaki. If you only read one article, read this one – and then join the efforts to make it a reality.

FRANK BARNABY
DOUGLAS HOLDSTOCK
Medicine and War
601 Holloway Road, London N19 4DJ

(15 June 1995)

References

1. Turco RP, Toon OB, Ackerman TP, Pollack JB, Sagan C. Nuclear winter: Global consequences of multiple nuclear explosions. *Science* 1983; **222**: 1283–1292.
2. Pittock AB *et al*. *Environmental consequences of Nuclear War. Vol. I: Physical and Atmospheric Effects*. Chichester: John Wiley, 1985.
3. Harwell MA, Hutchinson TC (eds). *Environmental Consequences of Nuclear War. Vol. II: Ecological and Agricultural Effects*. Chichester: John Wiley, 1985.
4. Hersey J. *Hiroshima*. New York: Knopf, 1946/Harmondsworth: Penguin, 1966.
5. Prins G. Public medicine and global security. *Medicine and War* 1992; 8: 241–258.
6. Sagan C, Turco RP. Nuclear winter in the post-cold-war era. *Journal of Peace Research 1993*; **30**: 369–373.
7 International Physicians for the Prevention of Nuclear War. *Radioactive Heaven and Earth*. New York: Apex Press/London: Zed Books, 1991.
8. Caldicott H. *Nuclear Madness: What You Can Do!*. Brookline, Mass.: Autumn Press, 1978: 11.
9. Gorbachev M. *Perestroika*. London: Collins, 1987: 154.

HIROSHIMA AND NAGASAKI

Part I

THE PAST
HIROSHIMA AND NAGASAKI:
THE BOMBINGS AND THEIR AFTERMATH

The Effects of the Atomic Bombings of Hiroshima and Nagasaki

FRANK BARNABY

8:15 am – atomic bomb released – 43 seconds later, a flash – shock wave, craft careens – huge atomic cloud

9:00 am – cloud in sight – altitude more than 12,000 metres

This is an extract from the log-book of the *Enola Gay*, the B-29 bomber which dropped the atomic bomb which obliterated Hiroshima on 6 August 1945. At 11.02 a.m. on 9 August 1945 a second atomic bomb destroyed the city of Nagasaki.

The Two Atomic Bombs

The atomic bomb exploded about 600 metres above the centre of the city with an explosive power equivalent to that of 12,000 tonnes of TNT. This huge explosion, more than a thousand times more powerful than the largest conventional bomb (called the earthquake bomb!), was obtained by the nuclear fission of a mere 700 grams of uranium-235, out of the 60 kilograms or so of uranium-235 in the atomic bomb, which was called 'Little Boy', an early example of the way names are used to make nuclear weapons sound less horrific and more acceptable. Little Boy was, by today's standards, a crude device, nearly 3 metres in length and weighing about 4 tonnes.

The atomic bomb used to destroy Nagasaki was called 'Fat Man'. It had an explosive power equivalent to that of about 20,000 tonnes of TNT. Plutonium-239 was the fissile material used in Fat Man; about 1.3 kilograms were fissioned out of the 6 kilograms or so in the bomb. Fat Man was about 3 metres long, 1.5 metres wide, and 4.5 tonnes in weight.

In comparison, a modern nuclear warhead, like the Minuteman III Intercontinental Ballistic Missile, weighs only about 150 kilograms and has an explosive power equivalent to that of 350,000 tonnes of TNT. Nuclear weapon scientists have made staggering advances in nuclear warhead design.

Since 1945 approximately 128,000 nuclear weapons have been built; about 70,000 by the United States, 55,000 by the Soviet Union, 1,100 by France, 850 by the United Kingdom, and 600 by China. In addition, Israel is thought to have about 150 nuclear weapons; India and Pakistan are each thought to have some nuclear weapons.

The Numbers Killed

Hiroshima is built on a plateau and the city was damaged symmetrically in all directions. Nagasaki is built on mountainous ground and the damage varied considerably according to direction. But the number of people killed at given distances from the hypocentre – the point on the ground directly below the centre of the exploding bomb – was roughly the same in both cities.

Almost all of those within 500 metres of the hypocentres when the atomic bombs exploded were dead by the end of 1945. About 60 per cent of those within 2 kilometres died; about three-quarters of them in the first 24 hours.

The number of people in Hiroshima when the atomic bomb exploded is not very well known. Tens of thousands of troops and Korean forced labourers were there, for example, but the exact number is not known. The best estimate is that the total number of people in the city was about 350,000.

The number of people killed is also not well known. The number who initially survived but died in the following few years from the effects of the bomb is not known; nor is the fate of the 37,000 or so people who came into Hiroshima within the first week of the bombing. The best estimate is that 140,000 Hiroshima citizens had died by the end of 1945. Many thousands of people were reported missing in the 1950 National Census, so that even this large figure may be an underestimate.

About 280,000 people are thought to have been in Nagasaki when the atomic bomb exploded. According to the best estimate, roughly 74,000 were dead by the end of 1945. There were many Koreans in Nagasaki, too. The number killed is not known.

The total number of people killed by Little Boy and Fat Man probably exceeds 250,000, a staggeringly high death rate of more than 40 per cent. The exact number will never be known. For comparison, the bombing of Dresden in February 1945 killed about 35,000 people. But, whereas the Dresden air raid involved hundreds of heavy bombers, only one aircraft was used to destroy Hiroshima and Nagasaki.

The Effects of Blast and Fire

Those killed very quickly were either crushed or burnt to death. The combined effects of blast and thermal radiation were particularly lethal. Many of those burned to death in collapsed buildings would have escaped with only injuries if there had been no fires. But an area of 13 square kilometres in Hiroshima and 7 square kilometres in Nagasaki were reduced to rubble by blast and then to ashes by fire. The difference in area was mainly due to the different terrain.

About a half of the energy generated by the nuclear explosions was given off as blast. The front of the blast moved as a shock wave – a wall of air at high pressure spreading outward at a speed equal to or greater than the speed of sound. It travelled about 11 kilometres in 30 seconds. The shock wave was followed by a wind of hurricane force. As the shock wave travelled outward, the pressure behind fell below atmospheric pressure and eventually the air flowed in the inward direction. Thus, a supersonic shock wave was followed by an exceedingly powerful wind, and then, after an instant of deathly stillness, a violent wind blew in the opposite direction.

In Hiroshima, all buildings within 2 kilometres of the hypocentre were damaged beyond repair by a blast of up to 3 tonnes per square metre. Casualties due to blast were particularly severe within about 1.3 kilometres of the hypocentre where the blast produced a pressure of as much as 7 tonnes per square metre.

About one-third of the energy generated by the atomic bombs was given off as heat. The fireballs produced by the nuclear explosions very rapidly reached temperatures of the same magnitude as those in the Sun – several millions of degrees Centigrade. With a second of the explosion, the fireballs grew to their maximum diameters of about 300 metres; the surface temperatures of the fireballs were about 5,000 degrees Centigrade.

At a distance of 500 metres from the hypocentre in Hiroshima nearly 60 calories per square centimetre of thermal radiation were emitted in the first 3 seconds – a heat 900 times more searing than the heat from the Sun. Even at a distance of 3 kilometres from the hypocentre, the heat in the first 3 seconds was about 40 times greater than that from the Sun. The heat at Nagasaki was even more intense, roughly twice as intense as that at Hiroshima.

The heat was sufficient to burn exposed skin at distances as great as 4 kilometres from the hypocentres. Many people caught in the open within about 1.2 kilometres from the hypocentres were burnt to death; some were simply vaporized. Violent firestorms raged in Hiroshima and Nagasaki. The one in Hiroshima was particularly severe. It lasted for half a day, completely consuming every combustible object within 2 kilometres of the hypocentre. (Plates 1, 2, 3)

Hiroshima had about 76,000 buildings when the atomic bomb was dropped. Two-thirds of them were destroyed by fire. Nagasaki had about 51,000 when the atomic bomb was dropped. A quarter of them were completely destroyed and many more seriously damaged. In the midst of such extensive damage, effective fire-fighting was out of the question. In any case, there was no water.

But some rain fell. Moisture condensed around rising hot-ash particles as they came into contact with cold air. But the rain which fell on both cities was not clean rain but an odious liquid that was oily and highly radioactive. It was known as 'black rain'.

The Effects of Ionizing Radiation

About 15 per cent of the energy generated by the atomic bombs was given off as ionizing radiation. About a third of it was emitted within a minute of the nuclear explosions, known as the initial radiation. The remainder, called residual radiation, was emitted from radioactive isotopes.

The initial radiation dose at the hypocentre in Hiroshima was about 240 Grays (24,000 rads). In Nagasaki, the dose at the hypocentre was about 290 Grays. One-half of a large number of people exposed to a whole-body radiation dose of 4 Grays will die. Virtually all those exposed to whole-body radiation of 7 Grays or more will die quickly. Exposed people within about a kilometre of the hypocentres of the Hiroshima and Nagasaki atomic bombs are thought to have received radiation doses of about 4 Grays.

Those exposed to large doses of radiation generally rapidly became incapacitated, suffering from nausea and vomiting, the first symptoms of radiation sickness. They later typically vomited blood, developed a high fever, had severe diarrhoea and much bleeding from the bowels. They usually died an unpleasant death within 10 days or so.

Those exposed to smaller doses of radiation suffered a wide variety of symptoms, including nausea, vomiting, diarrhoea, and bleeding from the bowel, gums, nose, and genitals. There was often a total loss of body hair, fever, and a feeling of great weakness. Resistance to infection was considerably reduced. Septicaemia was a frequent cause of death. (Plate 4)

The Late Effects of Radiation Exposure

Most of the survivors alive at the end of 1945 appeared to be reasonably healthy. But later a variety of illnesses – such as eye diseases, blood disorders, psycho-neurological disturbances, and malignant tumours – began to appear. The delayed effects are the most terrifying consequences of the use of nuclear weapons.

Leukaemia among the survivors increased rapidly for about a decade after the bombings. The mortality rate for leukaemia reached a level of about 30 times higher than that of non-exposed Japanese. The incidence of other malignant tumours – thyroid, breast, lung, prostate, bone, salivary glands, and so on – has been higher among the survivors than among the non-exposed Japanese ever since the atomic bombs were dropped.

Children born to women pregnant when the atomic bombs exploded showed an increase in some congenital malformations, particularly microcephaly (abnormally small size of the head), resulting in mental retardation.

Surprisingly, there is an apparent absence of genetic effects in the survivors exposed to radiation from the atomic bombs. Animal experiments and other evidence show that radiation undoubtedly causes genetic

'Friends, Please Forgive Us'

Kataoka Osamu, a teenage schoolboy at the time, was in Hiroshima when the atomic bomb exploded. His account of the disaster is far more eloquent than any scientific description can be:

> I looked out of the window at the branch of a willow tree. Just at the moment I turned my eyes back into the old and dark classroom, there was a flash. It was indescribable. It was as if a monstrous piece of celluloid had flared up all at once. Even as my eyes were being pierced by the sharp vermilion flash, the school building was already crumbling. I felt plaster and roof tiles and lumber come crashing down on my head, shoulders, and back. The dusty smell of the plaster and other strange smells mixed up with it penetrated my nostrils.
>
> I wonder how much time passed. It had gradually become harder and harder for me to breathe. The smell had become intense. It was the smell that made it so hard to breathe.
>
> I was trapped under the ruins of the school building ... I finally managed to get out from under the wreckage and stepped out into the schoolyard. It was just as dark outside as it had been under the rubble and the sharp odour was everywhere. I took my handkerchief, wet it, and covered my mouth with it.
>
> Four of my classmates came crawling out from beneath the debris just as I had done. In a daze we gathered around the willow tree, which was now leaning over. Then we began singing the school song. Our voices were low and raspy, with a tone of deep sadness. But our singing was drowned out by the roar of the swirling smoke and dust and the sound of the crumbling buildings.
>
> We went to the swimming pool, helping a classmate whose leg had been injured and who had lost his eyesight. You cannot imagine what I saw there. One of our classmates had fallen into the pool; he was already dead, his entire body burned and tattered. Another was trying to extinguish the flames rising from his friend's clothes with the blood which spurted out of his own wounds. Some jumped into the swimming pool to extinguish their burning clothes, only to drown because their badly burned limbs had become useless. There were others with burns all over their bodies whose faces were swollen to two or three times their normal size so they were no longer recognizable. I cannot forget the sight of those who could not move at all, who simply looked up at the sky, saying over and over, 'Damn you! Damn you!'
>
> Our gym teacher had come to the swimming pool, too. Though he was moving about energetically, the sight of his burned and swollen body and his tattered clothes made everyone's heart sink. We all began to cry. But he gave us directions and encouraged us in a firm voice, urging us to gather together our friends who had lost their sight or were badly injured and to leave the burning school building behind.
>
> There were others who could not move at all and there were probably many who were still trapped beneath the burning ruins of the school. Were we to run away and leave them behind without caring at all? No. ... But there was nothing we could do, nothing. Friends, please forgive us.

Clinical descriptions of the medical effects of radiation cannot convey their magnitude as well as the words of someone who has experienced them. One such person was Futaba Kitayama, then a 33-year-old housewife, who was 1.7 km from the hypocentre of the Hiroshima bomb. She has described her experiences in a Japanese journal:

Someone shouted, 'A parachute is coming down!' I responded by turning in the direction she pointed. Just at that moment, the sky flashed. I do not know how to describe that light. I wondered if a fire had been set in my eyes.

I don't remember which came first – the flash of light or the sound of an explosion that roared down to my belly. Anyhow, the next moment I was knocked down flat to the ground. Immediately, things started falling down around my head and shoulders. I couldn't see anything; it seemed pitch dark. I managed to crawl out of the debris.

Soon I noticed that the air smelled terrible. Then I was shocked by the feeling that the skin of my face had come off. Then, the hands and arms, too. Starting from the elbow to the fingertips, all the skin of my right hand came off and hung down grotesquely. The skin of my left hand, all five fingers, also came off.

What happened to the sky that had been such a clear blue one only a moment ago? It was now dark, like dusk. I ran like mad toward the bridge, jumping over the piles of debris.

What I saw under the bridge was shocking: hundreds of people were squirming in the stream. I couldn't tell if they were men or women. They looked all alike. Their faces were swollen and grey, their hair was standing up. Holding their hands high, groaning, people were rushing to the river. I felt the same urge because the pain was all over my body which had been exposed to a heat ray strong enough to burn my pants to shreds. I was about to jump into the river when remembered that I could not swim.

I went back up to the bridge. There schoolgirls, like sleepwalkers, were wandering about in confusion.

When crossing the bridge, which I did not then recognize, I found all its parapets of solid ferro-concrete had gone. It looked terribly unsafe. Under the bridge were floating, like dead dogs or cats, many corpses, barely covered by tattered clothes. In the shallow water near the bank, a woman was lying face upward, her breasts torn away and blood spurting. A horrifying scene. How in the world could such a cruel thing happen? I wondered if the Hell that my grandmother had told me so much about in my childhood had fallen upon the Earth.

I found myself squatting in the centre of the parade ground. It could not have taken me more than two hours to get there. The darkness of the sky abated somewhat. Still, the Sun, as if covered with a heavy cloud, was dim and gloomy.

My burns started paining me. It was a kind of pain unlike that of an ordinary burn which might be unbearable. Mine was a dull pain that was coming from somewhere far from my body. A yellow secretion oozed from my hands. I imagined that my face also had to be in this dreadful condition. By my side, many junior high school students were squirming in agony.

They were crying insanely, 'Mother! Mother!' They were so severely burned and blood-stained that one scarcely dared look at them. I could do nothing for them but watch them die one by one, seeking their mothers in vain.

As far as I could see with my failing eyesight all was in flames.

Steadily, my face became stiffer. I put my hands carefully on my cheeks and felt my face. It seemed to have swollen to twice its normal size. Now I could see less and less. Soon I would not be able to see at all. I kept walking. I saw on the street many victims being carried away by stretcher. Carts and trucks, loaded with corpses and wounded who looked like beasts, went by. On both sides of the street, many people were wandering about like sleepwalkers.

damage. Among the reasons suggested by experts for the absence of genetic damage in the atomic-bomb survivors are: the methods used to search for genetic effects are insufficiently sensitive; there may have been a large number of spontaneous abortions; and the number of survivors involved, and the radiation doses received by them, are such that too few of the children examined showed genetic effects to be statistically significant, even though these may have been present. The absence of observed genetic abnormalities in survivors of the atomic bombings certainly does not mean that exposure to radiation does not produce genetic damage.

Social Effects of the Atomic Bombings

The social and psychological effects of the atomic bombings were very severe. The communities in Hiroshima and Nagasaki disintegrated and the social services collapsed. Many people went mad or committed suicide. Thousands of children became orphans.

Fear of malformed offspring often prevented marriage. Unusual susceptibility to disease and fatigue often threatens employment. The ratio of sick or injured among the survivors was almost twice the national average.

A tragic after-effect of the atomic bombings is the fear in young off-spring of the survivors that they may develop some dread disease, like cancer, because their parents were exposed to radiation. These young people also fear that they may give birth to deformed babies because of the experience of their parents, or even grandparents. This effect on the innocent is one of the most tragic, and most frequently overlooked, consequences of the use of nuclear weapons.

(15 April 1995)

Frank Barnaby worked as a physicist at the Atomic Weapons Research Establishment, Aldermaston (1951–57). He was on the senior scientific staff, Medical Research Council and Lecturer at University College London from 1957 to 1967. He has been Executive Secretary of the Pugwash Conferences on Science and World Affairs (1969–70), Director of the Stockholm International Peace Research Institute (1971–81), Guest Professor at the Free University, Amsterdam (1981–85) and Visiting Professor, Stassen Chair at the University of Minnesota (1985). He is currently a defence analyst and writer on military technology.

His many books include: *The Invisible Bomb, The Gaia Peace Atlas, The Automated Battlefield, Star Wars, Future Warfare, Verification Technologies, Man and the Atom, Nuclear Energy,* and *Prospect for Peace.* He has published numerous articles on military technology and defence and disarmament issues in scientific journals, newspapers, and magazines.

Correspondence: 'Brandreth', Station Road, Chilbolton, Stockbridge, Hants SO20 6AW.

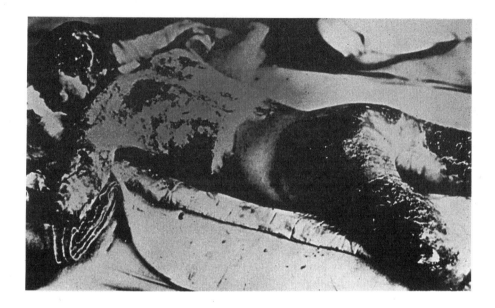

PLATE 1. Man with total body burns.

PLATE 2. Human silhouette imprinted on surface of steps.

PLATE 3. Hiroshima: the firestorm.

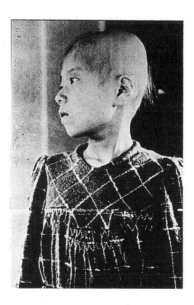

PLATE 4. Girl in severe hair epilation stage after radiation exposure.

Hiroshima and Nagasaki: The Beginning of the Nuclear Age

KAZUYO YAMANE

Were there Alternatives to the Atomic Bombings?

The controversy over the Smithsonian *Enola Gay* exhibition implies that it is still taboo to question the United States' use of the atomic bomb. Veterans' groups and conservatives succeeded in using the exhibit to justify and glorify the use of the atomic bomb. Historical facts, however, suggest a different reality: the use of the atomic bomb was not necessary to end the war.

The Japanese government made overtures for peace before the Potsdam Conference. They were ignored; Hiroshima and Nagasaki were bombed. The following is a summary of the course of Japan's plea for peace, based on the Japanese Foreign Ministry publication *A Record of the History of World War II*.[1]

Japan's Pre-Potsdam Conference Peace Proposal

11–14 May 1945	The Supreme War Direction Council of Japan held a meeting and decided to ask the Soviet Union to act as a mediator to end the war.
12 July	The Emperor asked Prince Konoye to be a special emissary to the Soviet Union (USSR). When Konoye accepted, Foreign Minister Togo sent a telegram to Ambassador Sato in Moscow to negotiate to end the war with Russia's help.
13 July	Ambassador Sato tried, but was unable, to meet the Russian foreign minister. He subsequently met the deputy foreign minister and gave him the Emperor's message.
16 July	The success of the first nuclear test was reported to President Truman in Potsdam.
17 July	The Potsdam conference lasted until 2 August. During the conference Stalin showed Truman a copy of the Emperor's message; and asked for his advice. Truman advised Stalin not to recognize Konoye as a special emissary.[2] (An adviser and an interpreter for the US Department of State recorded this conversation).[3]

18 July	Russia responded to Japan on the Konoye mission, saying that the Soviet Union would not accept the Japanese proposal.
21 July	Foreign Minister Togo sent Ambassador Sato a telegram instructing him again to ask the Soviet Union to help mediate an end to the war.
25 July	Sato met the Soviet Deputy Foreign Minister and gave him Togo's message. The Deputy Foreign Minister promised to pass it on to his government. On the same day, foreign minister Togo sent Sato a further telegram, instructing him to meet with the Soviet Foreign Minister because he understood that Churchill and Attlee would return to England on the 26th, when the Potsdam conference was to be adjourned.[1]
	In Washington a document authorizing the use of the atomic bomb was issued on the 25th. (Why was the order issued on this date? It should have been issued after a Japanese rejection of the Potsdam Declaration Ultimatum.)
26 July	The Potsdam Declaration Ultimatum.
28 July	Japan rejected the Potsdam Declaration Ultimatum.
6 August	The uranium bomb was dropped on Hiroshima.
8 August	Russia declared war on Japan.
9 August	The plutonium bomb was dropped on Nagasaki.
14 August	Japan accepted the Potsdam Declaration Ultimatum.
15 August	Japan surrendered, bringing the Second World War to an end.

Although Japan tried to end the war through discussions with the Soviet Union, the proposal was not considered seriously by the United States and USSR. Japan might have surrendered more quickly if the United States had softened its insistence on unconditional surrender and had assured the Japanese that the Emperor would be able to keep his throne.

What was the attitude of the British Prime Minister, Winston Churchill? According to *No High Ground*,[4] Churchill and Truman agreed on the decision to use atomic weapons against Japan on 4 July. In discussing this decision, Nishijima cites the following statement by Churchill:[2]

British consent in principle to the use of the weapon had been given on July 4, before the test had taken place. The final decision now lay in the main with President Truman, who had the weapon; but I never doubted what it would be, nor have I ever doubted since that he was right. The historic fact remains, and must be judged in the after-time, that the decision whether or not to use the atomic bomb to compel the surrender of Japan was never even an issue. There was unanimous, automatic, unquestioned agreement around our table; nor did I ever hear the slightest suggestion that we should do otherwise.[5]

Churchill did not consider an alternative way of ending the war. Attlee, his successor as Prime Minister of the United Kingdom, stated that Japan's offer of peace was not accepted at Potsdam, further substantiated in *Hansard* for 19 December 1946.[6] The Potsdam Conference ignored the Japanese overtures for peace.

Why Did Truman Use the Atomic Bombs?

The United States was aware of Japan's move for peace because it was intercepting and decoding the messages Foreign Minister Togo was sending to Ambassador Sato.[4] Why did Truman advise Stalin to ignore Japan's plea for peace on 17 July? Perhaps he was afraid of losing an opportunity to use the atomic bombs, which had cost $2 billion to develop and produce.[2] Another question is why Truman used the atomic bomb before 8 August when Russia declared war against Japan. According to *The Dictionary for Practising Peace Education*, the United States wanted to display its power to the Soviet Union to exclude it from taking part in the settlement of post-war issues in East Asia.[7] Nishijima pointed out that 'the atomic bombs were regarded not only as military weapons, but also political weapons whose great power would make Russia obey to the United States even before the bombs were made'.[2] This is why Truman ignored, and even concealed, the Japanese proposal for peace.

Gar Alperovitz insisted that there was no need for the use of the atomic bombs in this way:

> It is clear that alternatives to the bomb existed and that Truman and his advisers knew it … Why then were the atomic bombs used? … Some writers also suggest that because huge sums were spent developing the new weapon, the US political leadership found it impossible not to use it. Most relevant to the Smithsonian flap is substantial scholarly acceptance of the once controversial idea that diplomatic issues – especially the hope of strengthening the West's hand against the Soviet Union – played a significant role in the decision.[8]

The Japanese were guinea pigs for the first 'live' nuclear weapon experiments with two types of atomic weapon, using uranium and plutonium.

The Aftermath of Hiroshima and Nagasaki

The book *Days to Remember*[9] cites statistics from the 1977 Non-Governmental Organizations Symposium on Atomic Destruction Report. From 310,000 to 320,000 civilians and more than 40,000 soldiers in Hiroshima were directly exposed to the heat, blast, and radiation released by the atomic bomb. The number exposed in Nagasaki was between 270,000 and 280,000. In Hiroshima, 92 per cent of the buildings were destroyed by the blast and fire, and in Nagasaki more than one third of the buildings were destroyed, over an area of about 6.7 square kilometres. The difference in the extent of damage relates to geographical difference: Hiroshima is a city on a flat delta surrounded by mountains, while Nagasaki is situated on mountainous terrain. The reality of the atomic bombings was the mass and instantaneous death of innocent civilians and the long-term suffering of those who survived. Over 300,000 survivors are still alive today. It is deplorable that the United States imposed press censorship on Japanese and foreign journalists in September 1945. A Japanese photographer, Shigeo Hayashi, took many photographs immediately after the bombings. All his film was confiscated by General Headquarters (GHQ) in December 1945.[10] Not until 1973, when the materials on the atomic bombings were returned to Japan, were his photographs given back. They are now exhibited in the Hiroshima Peace Memorial Museum. If there had been freedom of the press at that time, many journalists might have covered the event, publicizing the horror of atomic weapons and soliciting aid from outside Japan.

At this time the United States even obstructed aid from the International Red Cross. Masae Shinna, a Japanese lawer, stated that 'tens of thousands of victims could have been saved if there had been more relief supplies, including medicine from the Red Cross.'[11] The GHQ prohibited Japanese doctors from reporting the results of studies on atomic bomb victims in November 1945. These valuable records on the victims were confiscated and taken to the United States, decisively delaying the study and medical treatment of the atomic bomb survivors. In 1947 the Atomic Bomb Casualty Commission (ABCC) was founded in Hiroshima by the United States. Its purpose, however, was only to investigate 'the long-term bio-medical effects of radiation on the survivors of Hiroshima and Nagasaki.'[12] The treatment of victims was not included in the programme. All the information was taken to the United States without making it public in Japan.

Hibakusha Aid Law

After the US Bikini hydrogen bomb test explosion at Bikini in 1954, Japanese fishermen were exposed to radioactive fallout. This triggered a peace movement against the atomic and hydrogen bombs in Japan. The Japan Confederation of Atomic and Hydrogen Bomb Victims Organizations was founded in 1956 and demanded a *hibakusha* (victims of atomic and hydrogen bombs) aid law. The Medical Aid Law for victims of the nuclear weapons was established in 1957, 12 years after the atomic bombings. Most of the victims were unable to receive medical treatment when they really needed it, and lost their lives. Another law was established in 1968, but neither laws were adequate in meeting the needs of victims. Their diseases were unlike those caused by conventional weapons: keloids, cataracts, leukaemia, thyroid gland cancer, breast cancer and lung cancer, and so forth. Besides suffering from illness related to radiation, other common problems were loss of family and home, mental illness, and discrimination in employment and marriage. The victims subsequently repeatedly requested an aid law for *hibakusha*.

On 11 December 1994 the Diet finally ratified a bill to compensate financially the atomic bomb victims and their families. The bill includes comprehensive measures to support atomic bomb victims and grants of 100,000 yen (about £625) to those who are regarded as atomic bomb victims, or those who have lost family members from causes related to the atomic bombings prior to 1970. Its passage was the direct result of the peace movement in Japan against atomic and hydrogen bombs. Over ten million signatures were collected in support of the *Hibakusha* Aid Law; 75 per cent of local authorities passed resolutions supporting it.[13] The new law, however, does not include any references to the government's responsibility for the war, a long-time demand of the victims' groups.

According to the atomic bomb victims' organizations, there are three reasons why atomic bomb victims have demanded from the government an admission of responsibility for the war. One is that the Japanese government renounced its right to claim compensation from the United States in the San Francisco Peace Treaty in 1951, leaving the Japanese government responsible for compensation. The second reason is that Japan originally launched a war of aggression, and finally prolonged the war in an attempt to protect the imperial system: this led to the use of atomic weapons at the end of the war. Thirdly, the Japanese government ignored the atomic bomb victims for twelve years until the Medical Law was established in 1957, and even co-operated with the United States to conceal the extent of the devastation caused by the bombs. The *Hibakusha* Aid Law does not provide victims with sufficient monetary aid: they also require medical aid and pensions. Only 2,000 of the 330,000 victims are officially regarded as suffering from illnesses related to the atomic bombing. This is woefully inadequate, and leaves one to seek a further reason for the Japanese government's refusal to admit responsibility for the war. This seems to be related to current attitudes of the Japanese government towards nuclear issues.

References

1. The Japanese Foreign Ministry. *A Record of the History of World War II.* Tokyo: Rippoh Gyohsei Konwakai, 1993.
2. Nishijima A. *Why Were the Atomic Bombs Dropped?* Tokyo: Aoki Shoten, 1971.
3. Giovannitti L, Freed F. *The Decision to Drop the Bomb.* New York: Coward-McCann, 1965, Japanese edition: 197–8.
4. Knebel F, Bailey C. *No High Ground.* New York: Harper, 1960.
5. Churchill W. *The Second World War: Triumph and Tragedy.* Boston: Houghton Mifflin, 1953: 639.
6. *Hansard*, 19 December 1946, col. 418.
7. Hiroshima Institute for Peace Education. *The Dictionary for Practising Peace Education.* Tokyo: Rohdoh Junpohsha, 1981: 266.
8. Alperovitz G. 'Considering the A-bombs beyond the Smithsonian flap'. *The Daily Yomiuri*, 22 October 1994.
9. Hiroshima-Nagasaki Publishing Committee. *Days to Remember: An Account of the Bombing of Hiroshima and Nagasaki.* Tokyo: 1981: 36.
10. Hayashi S. *Entering the Blast Center in Hiroshima: What did a Photographer See?* Tokyo: Iwanami Shoten, 1992: 147–50.
11. Shinna M. *The Hibakusha Aid Law.* Tokyo: Iwanami Shoten, 1991: 29.
12. Lapenta J. 'Study in suffering from out of the ashes'. *The Daily Yomiuri*, 27 February 1995.
13. The Japanese Council against Atomic and Hydrogen Bombs. *A Demand for the Elimination of Nuclear Weapons and State Compensation for Hibakusha.* Tokyo: The Japanese Council against Atomic and Hydrogen Bombs, 1966: 12.

(20 March 1995)

Kazuyo Yamane is a part-time lecturer in Peace Studies at Kochi University. She is in charge of the International Exchange Section at Grass Roots House, a small peace museum in Kochi City, Japan. She has translated Japanese peace education materials into English, such as *Hiroshima: Living in This Nuclear Age* and *A Standard Curriculum For Peace Education* (Hiroshima Institute for Peace Education, 1980), and has published widely on peace education with particular reference to the role of peace museums.

Correspondence: Grassroots House, 9–11 Masugata, Kochi City 780, Japan.

The Acquisition of Nuclear Weapons

FRANK BARNABY

Nuclear weapons vary considerably in their complexity. The design of modern versions of the nuclear weapons which destroyed Hiroshima and Nagasaki would cause today's nuclear scientists and engineers no difficulty – virtually all the information required is in the open literature. The designers of this basic type of nuclear weapon would be so confident that their weapons would work that they would be satisfied with non-nuclear testing. The weapons could, therefore, be fabricated and deployed clandestinely.

Thermonuclear weapons, however, are much more complex. There are fewer details about their design in the open literature; designers would need access to sophisticated computers; and they would need nuclear testing before deployment. They could not, therefore, be deployed secretly.

Components of Nuclear Fission Weapons

If a country takes the political decision to manufacture a nuclear weapon force it must acquire or produce a wide range of components. The main components required to assemble a nuclear weapon which obtains all its explosive yield from nuclear fission (i.e., a nuclear-fission weapon or A-bomb) include:

- very high quality conventional high explosives;
- reliable detonators for these explosives;
- electronic circuits to fire the detonators in a precise time sequence;
- a tamper and a neutron reflector;
- a core of fissile material, preferably either weapon-grade plutonium or highly-enriched uranium; and
- a neutron source to initiate the fission chain reaction.

The smallest amount of fissile material which can sustain a fission chain reaction is called the critical mass. In a nuclear fission a sphere of plutonium or highly-enriched uranium weighing less than the critical mass is used. The sphere is surrounded by conventional high explosives which, when detonated, produce a shock wave which uniformly compresses the sphere, a technique called implosion.

The compression reduces the volume of the sphere and increases its density. The critical mass is inversely proportional to the square of the density. The original less-than-critical mass of fissile material will, after compression, become super-critical, a fission chain reaction will take place and a nuclear explosion take place.

Plutonium metal occurs in a number of phases, or crystalline forms, depending on how it is produced. For use in nuclear weapons, plutonium is usually alloyed with gallium. This makes it more machinable into precise shapes and prevents it changing from one phase to another. It is important to prevent a phase change because the new phase will have a different density. The volume of the plutonium will then change and the shape may distort.

Nuclear weapon designers prefer plutonium with a large concentration of the isotope plutonium-239 (Pu-239). Plutonium containing more than 93 per cent of Pu-239 is called weapon-grade plutonium. Plutonium which contains less Pu-239, and, therefore, higher concentrations of other plutonium isotopes, particularly Pu-240, presents the designer with problems. Pu-240 undergoes spontaneous fission and this heats up the mass of plutonium.

Also, the higher neutron flux may cause the weapon to detonate prematurely if precautions are not taken. Pre-detonation reduces the explosive power of the explosion. The critical mass of weapon-grade plutonium in the delta-phase, the type normally used, is 17 kilograms. The critical mass of alpha-phase weapon-grade plutonium is 10 kilograms. Delta-phase plutonium, however, is more stable and more easily compressed than alpha-phase.

The alternative to Pu-239 as the fissile material in nuclear weapons is uranium-235 (U-235). Weapon-grade highly-enriched uranium contains more than 90 per cent of U-235 and has a critical mass of about 56 kilograms. This is about four times greater than the critical mass of plutonium. However, the 'gun technique' can be used in a nuclear weapon using enriched uranium. In this design, a mass of uranium less than the critical mass is fired into another less-than-critical mass of uranium. The sum of the two masses is greater than critical. The gun design, which cannot be used with plutonium, is significantly simpler than the implosion design. (Figure 1)

In a nuclear weapon using the implosion design, the plutonium or highly-enriched uranium is typically surrounded by a spherical shell of beryllium to reflect back into the fissile material some of the neutrons which escaped through the surface of the sphere without causing fission. The use of a neutron reflector significantly reduces the amount of fissile material needed. The beryllium shell is surrounded, in turn, with a shell of a heavy material, like natural or depleted uranium, which acts as a tamper. The tamper is surrounded by the conventional high explosives. When the explosives are detonated, the shock wave causes the tamper to collapse inwards. Its inertia helps hold together the plutonium, for example, during the explosion to prevent the premature disintegration of the fissioning material and thereby obtain a larger explosion. (Figure 2)

The timing of the detonations of the chemical explosives to produce the

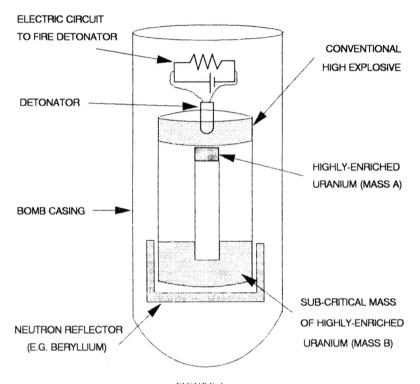

FIGURE 1
HIROSHIMA BOMB USING HIGHLY-ENRICHED URANIUM IN
GUN-TYPE DESIGN

The high-explosive charge drives the highly enriched uranium mass (A) at the top of the gun barrel down into the lower highly-enriched uranium mass (B). Mass A + Mass B is super-critical, whereas Mass A and Mass B are each less than critical. When A and B come together a nuclear explosion occurs.

shock wave is crucial for the efficient operation of the weapon. Micro-second (a millionth of a second) precision is essential. The shapes of the explosive segments (called explosive lenses) are rather complex and must be carefully calculated. The high explosive, such as HMX (cyclo-tetra-methylene-tetranitramine), must be chemically extremely pure and of con-stant constituency throughout its volume.

Normally, the more explosive lenses there are the more symmetrical the shock wave. Forty or so detonators would be typical. Getting the timing of the detonation sequence right is crucial – milli-microsecond (a thousandth of a millionth of a second) precision is required. For maximum efficiency, the fission chain reaction in a nuclear weapon must be initiated at precisely the moment of maximum super-criticality, i.e., the moment of maximum compression. The initiation is achieved by a burst of neutrons. In a

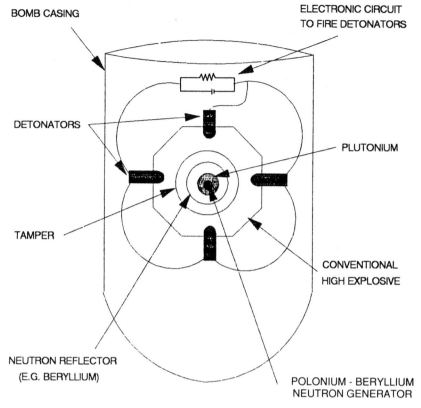

BOMB CASING

ELECTRONIC CIRCUIT
TO FIRE DETONATORS

DETONATORS

PLUTONIUM

TAMPER

CONVENTIONAL
HIGH EXPLOSIVE

NEUTRON REFLECTOR
(E.G. BERYLLIUM)

POLONIUM - BERYLLIUM
NEUTRON GENERATOR

FIGURE 2
NAGASAKI BOMB: IMPLOSION OF PLUTONIUM

The plutonium is a sub-critical mass. When conventional high-explosives are detonated, the plutonium sphere is compressed into a super-critical mass which explodes. The polonium-beryllium source is crushed by the explosion of the conventional high-explosive to produce a flux of neutrons to initiate the fission chain reaction.

modern weapon, the neutrons are produced by a small electronic device called a 'neutron gun' placed outside the conventional high explosives. A typical modern nuclear fission weapon would typically use three or four kilograms of weapon-grade plutonium surrounded by an efficient neutron reflector and tamper and about 100 or so kilograms of high explosive. The entire volume of the device would be about that of a football and its total weight roughly 200 kilograms.

In the nuclear explosion very high temperatures, of hundreds of millions of degrees centigrade, and very high pressures, of millions of atmospheres, build up in a very short time, about a half a millionth of a second. In this time, about 55 generations of fission take place. In less than a millionth of a second, the size and density of the fissile material have changed so that it becomes less than critical and the chain reaction stops.

The complete fission of one kilogram of Pu-239 would produce an explosion equivalent to that of 18,000 tonnes (18 kilotonnes or kt) of TNT. Modern fission weapons have efficiencies approaching 45 per cent, giving explosive yields of about 7 kt per kilogram of plutonium present.

Boosted Nuclear Fission Weapons

The maximum explosive power of a militarily usable nuclear fission weapon is about 50 kt. The explosive yield of a fission weapon can be enhanced (or 'boosted') by some nuclear fusion. But the explosive yield from a boosted weapon comes from nuclear fission. Nuclear fusion is used to produce more neutrons which, in turn, produce more fissions in the plutonium or highly-enriched uranium. Fusion produces an insignificant amount of energy.

In a boosted weapon, a mixture of tritium and deuterium gases are injected into the centre of the plutonium sphere of a nuclear fission weapon just after the fission process has begun, from a reservoir outside the main core of the weapon. When the fission weapon explodes, the temperature and pressure at centre are high enough for nuclear fusion to take place. The neutrons released during the fusion process produce additional fissions in the plutonium before the weapon disintegrates, increasing its efficiency.

In an unboosted fission weapon, the rate of production of fissions is about 100 per microsecond; in a boosted one, it is about 1,000 per microsecond. Boosted weapons are, therefore, about 10 times more efficient than unboosted ones. Militarily usable boosted weapons have explosive yields of up to 500 kt.

Thermonuclear Weapons

If nuclear explosions with explosive yields greater than a few hundred kilotonnes are required, extra energy must come from nuclear fusion. (In fission, heavy nuclei are split into lighter ones; in fusion, light nuclei are joined – i.e., fused – into heavier ones). In a thermonuclear weapon, or H-bomb, a significant fraction of the explosive yield comes from nuclear fusion.

A nuclear fission weapon is used in a thermonuclear weapon as a 'trigger' to provide the high temperature needed to produce nuclear fusion. Typically, tritium and deuterium are fused together to form helium. During the process, a neutron and energy are released. Because tritium and deuterium are gases at room temperature, it is convenient to use lithium-6 deuteride, a solid material, as the fusion material. A cylinder of lithium deuteride is placed under the nuclear fission trigger. When neutrons from the fission explosion bombard lithium-6 nuclei in the lithium deuteride, tritium nuclei are produced. These fuse with deuterium nuclei in the lithium deuteride to produce fusion energy.

In a typical thermonuclear weapon, a cylinder of highly-enriched uranium, known as the 'sparkplug', is placed co-axially with the cylinder of lithium deuteride. Neutrons from the trigger produce fission in the uranium sparkplug which ignite the fusion process. If higher explosive yields are required a second fusion stage can be placed under the first; in principle, other fusion stages can be added. Typically, each stage of a thermonuclear weapon explodes with a power roughly ten times that of the preceding stage. If the fission trigger explodes with an explosive yield of a few tens of kilotonnes, the first fusion stage will explode with a yield of several hundred kilotonnes, and the second fusion stage, if present, would yield several million tonnes (megatonnes, mt). For example, the Soviet Union exploded a four-stage thermonuclear weapon in 1962 with an explosive yield of 58 mt – equivalent to about 5,000 Hiroshima bombs.

The fusion process in a thermonuclear weapon is probably about 30 per cent efficient. If so, each kilogram of lithium-6 deuteride would produce an explosion equivalent to that of about 25 kt of TNT. A 500-kt weapon would require about 20 kilograms of lithium-6 deuteride.

Peaceful and Military Nuclear Programmes

There is a direct link between the proliferation of nuclear weapons and the spread of nuclear technology for peaceful purposes. Hannes Alfven, the Swedish Nobel Prize-winning nuclear physicist, described the peaceful and military atoms as 'Siamese twins'. Countries using nuclear power reactors to generate electricity or operating research reactors will inevitably acquire the necessary technical knowledge and scientific and engineering expertise to fabricate nuclear weapons. The 25 non-nuclear-weapon countries operating nuclear power reactors will also inevitably accumulate plutonium in spent reactor fuel elements which could be used for the construction of nuclear weapons.

Some elements of the nuclear fuel cycle are considerably more proliferation sensitive than others. Uranium enrichment plants and reprocessing plants, used to remove chemically the plutonium in spent reactor fuel elements, are particularly sensitive.

Large commercial reprocessing plants are currently operating in the United Kingdom, France, and Russia; one is under construction in Japan. Smaller plants are currently operating in India and Japan. A typical modern commercial reprocessing plant will reprocess about 800 tonnes of spent reactor fuel a year, separating out about 8 tonnes of plutonium a year.

The plutonium produced in a nuclear power reactor operated normally for the generation of electricity, known as reactor-grade plutonium, can be used to fabricate nuclear weapons, although nuclear-weapon designers would prefer weapon-grade plutonium. Reactor-grade plutonium typically contains about 60 per cent of Pu-239. The critical mass of reactor-grade plutonium metal in the delta-phase is about 20 kilograms; for alpha-phase it is 13 kilograms.

Current Stocks of Military and Civil Fissile Materials

Very little official information has been released by the nuclear weapon powers about the amounts of military fissile materials – plutonium and highly-enriched uranium – that they have produced. In fact, the only exception is the information recently released by the US Secretary of Energy, Hazel O'Leary, who said that the amount of military plutonium so far produced in the United States was 102 tonnes. The US Department of Energy admits, however, that it is simply unable to estimate the amount precisely – the actual amount could range up or down by as much as one or two tonnes. No other nuclear weapon power has given any figures at all.

There is also a lack of transparency about stocks of civil fissile material, particularly plutonium. One problem is that the operators of civil nuclear power plants are unable to measure directly the amount of plutonium produced in their nuclear power reactors. All they can do is to try to calculate the amount of plutonium in their spent reactor fuel elements from estimates of the burn-up of the reactor fuel. These calculations are bound to contain inaccuracies. Also, standards of material accountancy in nuclear facilities vary considerably. For these reasons, the figures given below for stocks of civil and military fissile materials are 'guesstimates' rather than precise amounts.

Civil and Military Plutonium

Currently, the world's total stock of plutonium, civilian and military, is about 1,100 tonnes (excluding the plutonium in the cores of the world's nuclear power reactors). Of this, about 800 tonnes are civil plutonium. The world's nuclear-power reactors are currently producing about 60 tonnes of plutonium a year; by the year 2000 the total amount of plutonium in the world will be about 1,400 tonnes. There are about 260 tonnes of military plutonium in the world's stockpile. A small amount of military plutonium is still being produced in Russia in reactors also used for domestic heating purposes. No military plutonium is being produced in the United States. The United Kingdom and France have more plutonium than they need for planned military purposes. The amount of military plutonium that China plans to produce in the future is not publicly known. India and Israel are probably still producing plutonium but in relatively small amounts. The world's stock of military plutonium is, therefore, unlikely to increase very much.

Currently, about 140 tonnes of civil plutonium have been separated from spent nuclear power reactor fuel elements in reprocessing plants. An additional 30 tonnes are being reprocessed a year so that by the end of 1998 there will be as much separated civil plutonium as military plutonium.

The amount of military plutonium in the United States is about 102 tonnes. About 40 tonnes of this plutonium are outside nuclear weapons. The United States is currently dismantling about 2,000 nuclear weapons a year, probably containing about 7 tonnes of plutonium. The amount of military plutonium in the former Soviet Union is probably about 120 tonnes. The amount outside weapons is probably about 50 tonnes. Russia is apparently dismantling about 1,800 nuclear weapons a year, probably containing about 7 tonnes of plutonium.

The United Kingdom has probably produced about 10 tonnes of military plutonium of which about 3 tonnes are in weapons. France may have produced roughly 6 tonnes of military plutonium of which about 2 tonnes are in nuclear weapons. China probably has much less in its weapons – perhaps about 2 tonnes. Israel may have produced about 800 kilograms of military plutonium and India about 300 kilograms.

It is reasonable to assume that about 100 tonnes of the world's 260 tonnes of military plutonium are currently outside nuclear weapons and that about 14 tonnes are added a year from dismantled nuclear weapons. By the year 2000, the total amount of military plutonium outside nuclear weapons may have increased to about 170 tonnes, or about 70 per cent of the world's total military plutonium. If this surplus military plutonium remains outside international safeguards it will, to say the least, considerably reduce the effectiveness of a fissile material cut-off treaty. Similarly, given that the world stock of separated civil plutonium will exceed the world stock of military plutonium by the end of 1998 and that this civil plutonium is usable in nuclear weapons, a fissile material cut-off treaty will be ineffective if it excludes civil plutonium.

Highly-Enriched Uranium

The situation with highly-enriched uranium is different from that with plutonium. The bulk of the world's stock of highly-enriched uranium is military; only about 1.5 per cent is civil. Moreover, the highly-enriched uranium removed from dismantled weapons can be disposed of more easily by mixing it with natural or depleted uranium to produce low enriched uranium for nuclear power reactor fuel. Low enriched uranium is not usable in nuclear weapons. However, the situation is complicated by the fact that highly-enriched uranium is used to fuel nuclear-powered warships. But, because of the surplus of highly-enriched uranium, it is likely that spent naval-reactor fuel will be permanently disposed of in geological repositories.

There are about 1,400 tonnes of highly-enriched uranium in the world – about 550 tonnes in the United States; about 800 tonnes in the ex-Soviet Union; and about 40 tonnes, roughly equally divided between the United Kingdom, France and China. Pakistan has probably produced 200 kilograms of highly-enriched uranium and South Africa about 360 kilograms. Excluding highly-enriched uranium used to fuel naval reactors, about 600 tonnes are outside nuclear weapons and about 800 tonnes in them. On average, a nuclear weapon (using an implosion design) contains about 15 kilograms of highly-enriched uranium. The dismantling of nuclear weapons will produce about 30 tonnes of highly-enriched uranium a year in each of the United States and Russia. By the year 2000, about 900 tonnes of highly-enriched uranium will be outside nuclear weapons.

International Safeguards

Currently, less than 1 per cent of the world's stock of highly-enriched uranium is under international safeguards, clearly an extremely unsatisfactory situation. In comparison, about 30 per cent of the world's inventory of plutonium is under international safeguards. Although this is a higher percentage than that for highly-enriched uranium it is still unsatisfactory.

In this context, it should be noted that reprocessing plants, separating plutonium from spent reactor fuel elements, are very difficult facilities to safeguard. Even using the best available and foreseeable security technology, safeguards on a large commercial reprocessing plant will be only 97 or 98 per cent effective. This means that 2 or 3 per cent of the plutonium cannot be accounted for. In a typical plant, separating 7 tonnes of plutonium a year, 140 to 210 kilograms of plutonium a year will be unaccounted for and may go missing without the operators or the safeguards agency knowing. This amount of plutonium could produce ten or more nuclear explosives.

Weapon Usability of Civil Fissile Materials

So far as nuclear proliferation is concerned, the important fissile isotopes are uranium-235 (U-235) and plutonium-239 (Pu-239). A sphere of pure U-235 would have a critical mass (the minimum amount required to sustain a fission chain reaction) of 15 kilograms. With uranium enriched to 40 per cent U-235, the critical mass increases to 75 kilograms; with 20 per cent U-235, it is 250 kilograms. In practice, therefore, high concentrations of U-235 are needed for the manufacture of nuclear weapons. Apart from the highly-enriched uranium used to fuel some research reactors, civil enriched uranium is of no military significance. Nuclear power reactor fuel, for example, is typically enriched to between 3 and 6 per cent.

The Isotopic Composition of Various Types of Plutonium

There are various grades of plutonium, having different isotopic composi-
tions, according to the way in which the plutonium is produced.
Plutonium produced in commercial nuclear power reactors operated for
the most economical production of electricity is called reactor-grade plutonium. Plutonium produced in military plutonium-production reactors,
specifically for use in nuclear weapons, is called weapons-grade plutonium.

Reactor-grade plutonium can be used to fabricate nuclear weapons, as
proved when the Americans exploded such a weapon in 1962. Nuclear
weapon designers, however, prefer weapons-grade plutonium. This has less
of the isotope plutonium-240 (Pu-240) than reactor-grade plutonium. In
fact, the less Pu-240 there is the better pleased nuclear weapon designers
are.

The isotopic composition of reactor-grade plutonium (produced in
thermal-reactor fuel elements exposed to about 33,000 megawatt-days per
tonne of uranium fuel) is about 1.4 per cent plutonium-238 (Pu-238); 56.5
per cent Pu-239; 23.4 per cent Pu-240; 13.9 per cent Pu-241; and 4.8 per
cent Pu-242. Weapons-grade plutonium contains about 0.05 per cent
Pu-238; 93.0 per cent Pu-239; 6.4 per cent Pu-240; 0.5 per cent Pu-241;
and 0.05 per cent Pu-242. Plutonium produced in the blanket of a typical
fast-breeder reactor contains about 96 per cent Pu-239 and 4 per cent
Pu-240. The plutonium in typical MOX fuel contains about 2 per cent
Pu-238; 42 per cent Pu-239; 31 per cent Pu-240; 14 per cent Pu-241; and
11 per cent Pu-242. (MOX, or mixed-oxide, reactor fuel contains a
mixture of uranium and plutonium oxides.)

Critical Masses of Plutonium

The critical mass of plutonium is the minimum mass which can sustain a
nuclear fission chain reaction. A nuclear weapon contains just less than the
critical mass in the form of a sphere or shell. To explode the nuclear
weapon, the mass of plutonium is uniformly compressed, by exploding
conventional high explosives placed around it, so that it becomes greater
than critical (super-critical).

At the instant of maximum super-criticality, neutrons are fired into the
plutonium, from a neutron 'gun', to initiate the fission chain reaction. At
this instant, the density of the plutonium is roughly doubled and the
plutonium is liquefied. The critical mass of a sphere of reactor-grade
plutonium in metal form (in the alpha-phase, density = 19.0 grams per
cubic centimetre) is 13 kilograms. In nuclear weapons, plutonium metal in
the delta-phase (density = 15.8 grams per cubic centimetre) is normally
used. The critical mass of a sphere of this type of reactor-grade plutonium
is 20 kilograms.

For weapons-grade plutonium, the critical mass of a sphere of the alpha-phase metal 11 kilograms; for the delta-phase metal it is 17 kilograms. For plutonium produced in the blanket of a breeder reactor, the critical mass for alpha-phase metal is 10 kilograms; for delta-phase it is 16 kilograms.

Plutonium oxide (the form in which plutonium is normally stored) varies in density from 11.5 grams per cubic centimetre in the crystal form to 2.3 grams per cubic centimetre for uncompacted powder. For the former the critical mass of a spherical volume is about 35 kilograms; for the latter it is about 875 kilograms.

Whereas Pu-239 undergoes fission when it captures a neutron, Pu-240 undergoes fission spontaneously; it does not need an extra neutron. This means that in plutonium containing Pu-240 there is a flux of neutrons from spontaneous fission. For breeder-blanket plutonium, this is 40 neutrons per second per gram; for weapons-grade plutonium, it is 66 neutrons per second per gram; and for reactor-grade plutonium, it is 360 neutrons per second per gram.

The higher the number of spontaneous-fission neutrons the greater the probability that the weapon will pre-detonate and explode with an unpredictable explosive yield. However, this can be compensated for by using faster implosion to compress a subcritical mass to a supercritical one. The faster the implosion the more predictable the yield of the nuclear explosion.

Another difference is the amount of heat generated by the absorption of alpha particles: breeder-blanket plutonium generates about 1.7 watts per kilogram; weapons-grade plutonium generates about 2.5 watts per kilogram; and reactor-grade plutonium generates about 11 watts per kilogram.

Japan's Monju breeder reactor, for example, is likely to produce about 140 kilograms of fissile plutonium, about half of it in the blanket elements. Because the burn-up of these elements is low, the plutonium produced in them is ideal for the manufacture of extremely efficient nuclear weapons. If the blanket elements are reprocessed separately, Japan will have a stock of weapons-grade material. The 70 kilograms or so of weapon-grade plutonium produced per year by Monju is enough to produce about 20 nuclear weapons a year, with an explosive yield at least equal to that of the nuclear weapon that destroyed Nagasaki (equivalent to the explosive power of about 20,000 tons of TNT).

References

1. Cochran TB, Arkin WM, Norris RS, Hoenig MM. *Nuclear Weapons Databooks (Vols 1 to 4)*. Washington DC: Natural Resources Defense Council, 1987.
2. Albright D, Berkhout F, Walker W. *World Inventory of Plutonium and Highly Enriched Uranium 1992*. Oxford: Oxford University Press, 1993.
3. Mark JC. *Reactor-Grade Plutonium's Explosive Properties*. Washington DC: Nuclear Control Institute, 1990.

(15 May 1995)

Correspondence: Brandreth, Station Road, Chilbolton, Stockbridge, Hants SO20 6AW.

Part II

THE PRESENT
NUCLEAR THREATS TODAY

The Current Status of the Nuclear Arms Race

PAUL ROGERS

The Nuclear Arms Race in the Early 1980s

Following the breakdown in East–West relations in the late 1970s, consequent in part on the Soviet intervention in Afghanistan and the installation of the markedly hawkish Reagan administration in the United States shortly afterwards, there was a period of intense escalation of nuclear deployments by both superpowers. This affected most classes of nuclear weapons, involved quantitative increases and also qualitative improvements in capabilities and was accompanied by similar if smaller-scale developments in the middle-ranking nuclear powers.

By the mid-1980s the Soviet Union was in the midst of a comprehensive upgrading of its strategic nuclear weapons, with new intercontinental ballistic missiles (ICBMs) such as the SS-24 being tested, the world's largest ballistic missile submarine, the *Typhoon*-class, being completed, a supersonic strategic bomber, the *Blackjack*, undergoing tests, and a number of nuclear-armed air-launched cruise missiles under development. Most of the new ICBMs and submarine-launched ballistic missiles (SLBMs) being deployed carried multiple independently-targeted re-entry vehicles (MIRVs) and showed considerable improvements in accuracy over earlier systems.[1]

In the United States, the considerable increase in defence spending by the incoming Reagan administration after 1981 was yielding a range of results. Improvements in existing classes of ICBM were in progress, and the new 10-warhead M-X ICBM was undergoing tests. A small ICBM was being developed and four of the new *Ohio*-class ballistic missile submarines were operational, deployed with the new Trident SLBM. The US Air Force had successfully petitioned for the redevelopment of the B-1 strategic bomber, cancelled by the previous Carter administration, and prototype flights of the modified B-1B commenced in 1983. A substantial programme of development and deployment of over a thousand air-launched cruise missiles was under way.[2]

In addition to the modernization and expansion of strategic nuclear weapons, there was a similar process affecting intermediate-range weapons. A prime focus of public attention was over the deployment of the so-called Euromissiles, the Soviet SS-20 and the US cruise and Pershing missiles. The ground-launched cruise missile, being deployed in five West European countries, was seen as a symbol of a nuclear war-fighting stance by NATO, a part of its commitment to early first use of nuclear weapons. There was little doubt that the Warsaw Pact had broadly similar policies.

In addition to these many substantial nuclear systems, it was recognized that both superpowers were developing many new kinds of tactical nuclear weapon, and that these were deployed in many countries and on warships cruising in most of the world's waters.

By 1984 the United States was believed to have nearly 11,000 strategic nuclear warheads, and the Soviet Union just over 8,000, although the latter were generally more powerful. In addition, there were estimated to be at least 20,000 intermediate and tactical nuclear systems deployed or under development. The strategic nuclear arms race was such that strategic arsenals of both superpowers were expected to expand by at least 50% during the course of the late 1980s.

The quantitative nuclear arms race was accompanied by qualitative changes, the most important being the development of highly accurate multi-warhead missiles. Many analysts argued that this greatly increased instability, especially at a time of crisis, through the possibility of either or both superpowers developing disarming first-strike policies.[2] This was made worse by the development of ideas about strategic defence, the so-called Star Wars programme. First strike strategic missiles combined with missile defences were seen to be particularly destabilizing in time of crisis, likely to encourage each side to initiate a nuclear exchange, a process expressed colloquially as 'use them or lose them'.

In addition to the then superpowers, during the early 1980s the middle-ranking nuclear powers, Britain, France and China, were all involved in nuclear modernization and expansion. Britain was upgrading the Polaris submarine-launched ballistic missiles with the Chevaline warhead and was developing the Trident successor to Polaris, and France and China were developing new land and sea-based missiles.

There were also concerns over proliferation. Israel was credited with having a substantial nuclear arsenal, South Africa was believed to have a small nuclear force, and India had tested a device ten years earlier and was assumed to be developing a nuclear arsenal. There was particular concern over the development of regional nuclear arms races in Latin America between Brazil and Argentina, in South Asia between India and Pakistan and in East Asia between the Koreas and between Taiwan and China. There was also a suspicion that Middle East states, specifically Iraq and Egypt and possibly Iran, had nuclear weapons programmes under way. In short, a superpower nuclear arms race was in progress, middle-ranking nuclear powers were expanding their forces and there were concerns over proliferation.

A Process of Transition

The easing of Cold War tensions began early in the time of the Gorbachev administration from 1985 onwards. For about two years almost all of the significant initiatives came from the Soviet Union, especially a number of temporary nuclear test bans. An improvement in Soviet–American relations with the Reykjavik Summit in 1987 was followed by the successful implementation of the INF treaty towards the end of the decade. This involved the removal of all land-based intermediate-range missiles from the US and Soviet inventories and included the Euro-based cruise, Pershing and SS-20 missiles, a process of symbolic as well as military importance.

This was followed by the relatively rapid negotiation of the two START agreements, again a process of bilateral Soviet–American arms control, which put into reverse the previous expansion of strategic arsenals and also set severe limits on numbers of multi-warhead missiles. Britain, France and China were not parties to these treaties and their own strategic programmes were largely unaffected by the superpower developments.

During the early 1990s the collapse of the former Soviet Union was accompanied by the large-scale withdrawal of many tactical nuclear systems and their placing in storage pending dismantling. The substantial majority of all naval and army tactical nuclear forces were involved in this process. In the United States, the US Army relinquished all of its tactical nuclear weapons, including artillery and battlefield missiles, and the wide range of naval tactical weapons was reduced to a handful of nuclear-armed cruise missiles on submarines. This process also affected the middle-ranking powers, especially Britain, where the numbers of tactical forces were cut substantially, including the withdrawal of all army and navy tactical systems.

The effect of all the changes of the past decade may be summarized briefly. Provided that the START 2 agreement is fully implemented, US and Russian strategic arsenals will each reduce to about 3,500 warheads by the early part of the next decade, although each party is likely to maintain reserve forces of a similar number of weapons, together with several hundred tactical nuclear weapons.[3] Total active forces will be around 8,000, with several thousand in reserve, but this compares with perhaps 45,000 at the peak period of deployment in the mid-1980s. Britain, France and China are all likely to have smaller nuclear forces, but with modernization continuing.

Concerning proliferation, substantial progress was made in Latin America, where greatly improved relations between Argentina and Brazil resulted in an agreement to curb nuclear weapons developments. There was also evidence of a US success in limiting the nuclear ambitions of South Korea and Taiwan, although tensions remain over the status of North Korea. South Africa announced the dismantling of its small nuclear arsenal.

In the Middle East and South Asia, by contrast, there remain major concerns. Pakistan is now considered to be a nuclear-capable state, and it and India are both developing substantial missile capabilities as well as likely to have active nuclear weapons development programmes. One effect of the Gulf War was to demonstrate that Iraq had made much more progress in developing nuclear weapons than had been assumed, and Iran is believed to have a limited nuclear weapons development programme. Furthermore, Israel remains a substantial nuclear power, a matter of continuing concern to states such as Egypt.

The Nuclear Age – End or Transition?

It would seem from the foregoing description that the intense nuclear arms race between the two superpowers, developing in the late 1940s and lasting for forty years, is largely over. There have been significant agreements which have resulted in nuclear arms control and some nuclear disarmament. These have not just halted the trends towards quantitative and qualitative expansion of the nuclear arms race, but have, to an extent, put it into reverse.

There have also been significant decreases in the nuclear capabilities of the middle-ranking powers, a pronounced change of policy by a number of nuclear weapons states away from nuclear testing, and some progress on reversing regional nuclear aspirations, especially in Latin America. It is reasonable to conclude that the nuclear arms race of earlier decades is over in that form, and that some of the trends in nuclear proliferation have been curbed. It does not follow from these conclusions, though, that nuclear weapons are in process of wholesale withdrawal, nor that the international system is moving clearly towards a non-nuclear environment. There is, rather, strong evidence to indicate that the nuclear era is not over, but in a process of transition.

This is apparent from a number of trends. Within Russia, there are few indications of any willingness to consider moving beyond the planned START 2 limits. There are occasional references to the desirability of negotiating a START 3 agreement, but at the same time there are also indications of a process of limited nuclear modernization under way. Russia is divesting itself of much of its armed forces, with rapid cuts in naval, army and air forces, yet certain core types of force are being retained in substantial numbers. These include rapid deployment and long-range power projection forces, core naval and air forces, and substantial strategic nuclear forces. These latter include a programme of continuing strategic nuclear developments such as the testing of a new or heavily modified ICBM.[3]

Similarly, the United States is in the process of re-orientating all the major branches of its armed forces to maintain its security interests in what is now seen to be a disorderly and unstable world. This process includes significant developments in long-range air power, a commitment to rapid deployment, carrier strike power, amphibious and special operations forces. Furthermore, the United States is maintaining substantial nuclear forces and is developing new nuclear targeting options including the packaging of small nuclear 'expeditionary' forces for possible use in limited regional wars.[4]

Concerning nuclear weapons and policy, both Britain and France are following a broadly similar programme – nuclear forces primarily relevant to the East–West confrontation are being downgraded or withdrawn, while other forces appropriate for the post-Cold War world are under development.[5] Britain's Trident system is a case in point. Originally conceived as a system for use against the former Soviet Union, this was a long-range, accurate multi-warhead submarine-launched missile with a destructive capability well in excess of post-Cold War requirements. As Britain withdraws its tactical nuclear forces over the next decade, Trident is now to be transformed into a flexible 'sub-strategic' missile system capable of carrying a small-yield single warhead suited for limited nuclear use in regional conflicts.[6]

The indications are that military planners in the more powerful states of the North, especially those with nuclear weapons, see a continuing requirement for nuclear forces, not least because they do not believe it likely that nuclear proliferation will be controlled. Furthermore, nuclear proliferation is seen as one part of a larger problem, the spread of weapons of mass destruction including chemical and biological weapons, area impact munitions and ballistic missiles.

There is a further belief that the East-West polarization of the Cold War era is being replaced by a North–South polarization, principally between the wealthy industrialised states and a substantial number of relatively poor states. In this context, weapons of mass destruction are seen to provide the latter with a means of redressing the military imbalance. Thus, one post-Cold War assessment of threats to western security included:

- widening economic differentials between the North and South;
- impact of high technology weapons and weapons of mass destruction on the ability – and thus the willingness – of the weak to take up arms against the strong;
- use of force or of terrorism to attempt to redress grievances or resolve problems.[7]

It is this expectation of a new axis of confrontation which is largely at the root of current changes in military orientation, including a commitment to versatile, modernized nuclear forces. The implications are clear – the nuclear arms race in its old form may be over, but the nuclear age is merely in a period of transition, with no expectation on the part of the military that it is feasible to move to a nuclear-free world.

Questions of Security

An assessment emerges of a future global security environment dominated by a North–South confrontation. This is fuelled by the deepening socio-economic divisions between rich and poor, and by environmental limitations on development, and made more dangerous by the increasing availability of weapons of mass destruction.[8] The northern military response is, broadly, to see this as constituting a new set of security problems or 'threats', which require a military response, one that includes maintenance of weapons of mass destruction, especially versatile nuclear forces. That this outlook envisages the possibility of small-scale nuclear use in regional conflicts should not be too surprising, given the strongly-developed nuclear war-fighting postures of NATO and the Warsaw Pact during the Cold War.

More generally, it does not appear to address the core issues responsible for the new axis of confrontation, and is likely to exacerbate a process leading to a deeply unstable international system characterized by Brooks as:

> a crowded, glowering planet of massive inequalities of wealth buttressed by stark force yet endlessly threatened by desperate people in the global ghettoes of the underprivileged.[9]

Within the context of the military dimension, it can be argued that this new world disorder should receive a response which accentuates the continuing need for arms control, disarmament and demilitarization. Concerning weapons of mass destruction, this should include further rapid progress towards Russian–American agreements such as a START 3, also involving middle-ranking powers such as Britain, a Comprehensive Test Ban Treaty and extension of the nuclear-free zone concept, with the aim being to progress towards a nuclear-free world. Furthermore, implementation of the Chemical Weapons Convention should be paralleled by a substantially renegotiated Biological Weapons Convention and the initiation of arms control processes applied to conventional weapons of mass destruction such as cluster munitions, fuel-air explosives and multiple rocket launchers.

These processes stand little chance of success without efforts to address the core problems of North–South confrontation. Otherwise, they will be seen increasingly as attempts by the powerful northern states to maintain their existing socio-economic global dominance by preventing southern states from acquiring powerful military capabilities.

It is therefore essential to recognize that a constrained and divided global system requires us to redefine concepts of security to embrace the kinds of socio-economic co-operation likely to heal the current deep divisions, as well as to encourage environmental co-operation which will address the global environment problems now evolving. This implies radical changes in political and economic behaviour which would appear to have little prospect at present. Yet these are likely to be essential in order to avoid a highly unstable and conflict-ridden global system.

During the Cold War there was a small but definite risk of an East–West nuclear confrontation which would have constituted an immediate and unparalleled global disaster. The post-Cold War transition is giving rise to a greater risk of limited use of weapons of mass destruction, including nuclear weapons, a process likely to result in the acceptance of such use as a regular aspect of war. That prospect alone provides a powerful motivation to redefine concepts of security in order to make the transition to a genuinely peaceful world order.

References

1. Rogers P. *Guide to Nuclear Weapons, 1984–85*, University of Bradford, 1984.
2. Dando M, Rogers P. *The Death of Deterrence*. London: CND Publications, 1984.
3. Norris RS, Arkin WM. US Strategic Forces, end of 1994. *Bulletin of the Atomic Scientists* 1995; **51(1)**: 69–71.
4. Strategic Advisory Group of the Joint Strategic Target Planning Group. US Strategic Air Command. The role of nuclear weapons in the new world order. Reported in *Navy News and Undersea Technology*, Washington DC, 13 January, 1992.
5. Yost DS. Nuclear debates in France. *Survival*, 1994–95; **36**: 113–39.
6. Miller D. Britain Ponders Single-Warhead Option. *International Defence Review*, 1994; September: 45–51.
7. Barnett RW. Regional conflict: requires naval forces. *Proceedings of the US Naval Institute*, 1992; June: 28–33.
8. Tansey G, Tansey K, Rogers P (eds). *A World Divided: Militarism and Development After the Cold War*. New York: St Martin's Press, and London: Earthscan, 1994.
9. Brooks E. The implications of ecological limits to development in terms of expectations and aspirations in developed and less developed countries. In Vann A, Rogers P (eds). *Human Ecology and World Development*. London and New York: Plenum Press, 1974.

(27 April 1995)

Paul Rogers is Professor of Peace Studies and Head of the Department of Peace Studies at Bradford University in England. He trained originally as a biologist and later developed a research interest in resource conflict and the politics of North–South relations. He chaired the UK Alternative Defence Commission from 1984 to 1987 and has written several books on international peace and security issues including, with Malcolm Dando, a *Violent Peace: Global Security after the Cold War* (Brassey's, 1992).

Fifty Years after Nagasaki: Japan as Plutonium Superpower

SHAUN BURNIE

... for any nation that has done its homework, separated plutonium –
in either metallic or oxide form – can be suddenly appropriated from
its storage place and inserted in warheads within days ... There is no
escape from the fact that any nation with a store of separated plutonium is a nation with a nuclear option that can be picked up at will
and on short notice.[1]

With the anniversary of the atomic bombing of Japan, and in particular
the use of plutonium to destroy Nagasaki, the world is reminded of the
destructive power of nuclear material. It is therefore tragically ironic that
fifty years after demonstrating its destructive capacities on the people of
Japan, the same country is embarked on a nuclear programme that will
make it a plutonium superpower before the end of the century. Whereas
the bomb that destroyed Nagasaki contained around 6 kilograms of plutonium, within ten years Japan will have more than 50,000 kilograms of
weapons-usable plutonium. This chapter summarizes the scale of Japan's
plutonium programme and in particular the threat that such a programme
will be used for military purposes.

Japanese Plutonium: Overseas Contracts and Domestic Production Facilities

Japan's plutonium programme consists of contracts held between Japanese
electrical utilities and European reprocessing companies on the one hand,
and domestic facilities both operating and under construction on the other.
The parallel development of a domestic plutonium infrastructure, combined with large-scale overseas reprocessing contracts, is unique to Japan,
and underscores the potential scale of the potential threat posed by its
plutonium programme.

From the 1970s onwards, nuclear reactor spent fuel was shipped from
Japanese light water reactors (LWRs) to Europe. By the end of 1995, more
than 5,000 tonnes in total will have been sent to the Sellafield site in the
United Kingdom and Cap de La Hague in France. Eventually all of it will
be reprocessed, yielding around 49–50 tonnes of plutonium. The storage
of the fuel in Europe served Japan's interests in several important ways. In
the first instance it removed temporarily the radioactive waste problem for
reactor operators, at a time in Japan when nuclear power expansion was

most rapid. Secondly, the reprocessed plutonium was intended to fuel Japan's commercial Fast Breeder Reactor (FBR) programme, thus allowing Japan to 'recycle' the plutonium. However, since the 1970s, Japan's FBR plans have been delayed. Most importantly the prototype Monju FBR only began operation in April 1994 after a multi-year delay. Plans for the next demonstration FBR have been postponed by 10 years, with likely further delays into the next century. It is now clear that Japan's ability to consume LWR plutonium in its FBR programme was overly optimistic, with the consequence of a massive surplus that will continue to grow. In an attempt to reduce this problem, as well as to gain further experience in plutonium fuel production and use, Japan has decided to use plutonium MOX in LWRs. Again, however, this will be a slow process requiring special licensing, and if experience in other countries is anything to go by, it will not proceed as currently anticipated by the authorities.

Domestic Facilities

Japan presently operates one plant for the reprocessing of nuclear fuel at Tokai-mura. Commissioned in 1981, this facility has the capacity to reprocess 210 tonnes of spent oxide fuel per year. However, operating experience has limited processing to around 40 tonnes of spent fuel annually. Figures provided by the operators of the reprocessing plant, the Power Reactor and Nuclear Fuel Development Corporation (PNC), a semi-autonomous government agency, report an annual production of 0.4 tonnes of plutonium. Authoritative calculations, however, show this to be an underestimate. In fact, a more accurate figure would be approximately 0.51 tonnes per year.

It is significant that operation of the Tokai facility was originally opposed by the United States administration under Presidents Ford and Carter in the late 1970s, as a result of US opposition to civilian reprocessing in an attempt to prevent nuclear weapons proliferation. Due to US opposition the Japanese government agreed to limit the production capabilities of Tokai, but this was reversed two years into the operation of the plant.

Japan plans to operate a larger, 800-tonnes per year, reprocessing plant at Rokkasho-mura, in northern Honshu, in an attempt to free itself from its current practice of shipping its spent nuclear fuel to Europe for reprocessing. After inevitable programme delays, construction of the facility is under way in spring 1995, with an operational date early next century. The plant will be capable of separating up to 7 tonnes of plutonium annually, all of it weapons-usable. Rokkasho-mura is intended to be the commercial centre of Japan's entire fuel cycle, where, in addition to plutonium fuel services, large-scale uranium enrichment and waste storage operations will be based.

In addition to LWR reprocessing plants, Japan also intends to operate facilities for the reprocessing of FBR reactor spent fuel, and the plutonium produced or 'bred' in the reactor blankets. As part of the first stage of this scheme, construction began in January 1995 of the Recycle Equipment Test Facility, or RETF. This test facility will only reprocess a relatively small amount of plutonium in total: however, that is not its significance. The most important aspect of the RETF is that it and the facilities that will follow will give Japan access to plutonium that is even purer than weapons-grade. The reason for this is that the plutonium produced in the uranium blanket of FBRs and reprocessed by the operators is what is called supergrade. With the large scale development of FBRs in Japan, and the reprocessing facilities to support the reactors, large quantities of weapons-grade material will be available for non-peaceful use. The fact that major components to be incorporated into the RETF were developed in the United States at nuclear weapons production facilities, further underlines the interrelationship between Japan's 'peaceful' plutonium programme and nuclear weapons.[2]

The PNC also operates the Tokai-mura plant for the production of MOX fuel – a mixture of plutonium and uranium oxides. The Tokai facility has a capacity to fabricate 5 tonnes of MOX per year for use in FBRs. Also to be built and operation by the late 1990s is a large-scale MOX plant, capable of fabricating 200 tonnes of plutonium fuel each year, to be built at the Rokkasho site. The argument used by Japanese industry is that MOX presents less of a security threat, despite MOX being classified as Category One material by the International Atomic Energy Agency (the same as plutonium), and requiring the highest level of protection. Plutonium contained within MOX fuel assemblies is easily removable and, therefore, represents a serious proliferation risk. Plutonium concentrations greater than 4 per cent within MOX would allow the material to be used in nuclear weapons. At higher concentrations of plutonium, MOX can even be used directly in nuclear devices. Chemical separation from the uranium would not be necessary (Frank Barnaby, personal communication).

Current and Future Plutonium Stockpiles

As already mentioned, Japan's plutonium programme has already led to an excess stockpile. As of late 1994, Japan's total plutonium inventory was reported to be 11 metric tonnes of separated material, an increase of 2.5 tonnes over 1993.[3] Eighty per cent, or 8,800 kilograms, of the 1994 total is surplus to current demands. Already Japan finds itself in the position, along with Germany, as having the largest stock of weapons-usable plutonium outside the nuclear weapon states. As European reprocessing of Japanese fuel proceeds through the 1990s, it is inevitable that the level of Japan's excess stockpile will grow to major proportions. On a realistic assessment of Japan's demand and supply situation in the next 15 years, it can be estimated that out of a total reprocessed stock of as much as 110 tonnes, as much as 80–85 tonnes will be surplus. To put this in perspective, Japan's total stockpile will be almost 25 per cent greater than is contained in the entire United States nuclear weapons arsenal. Only the former Soviet Union has more plutonium, and if Japan's programme continues into the mid-decades of the twenty-first century even that will be surpassed. The question that arises from the scale of Japan's programme is whether it be used for nuclear weapons.

Safeguards and the International Atomic Energy Agency

The most important technical barrier for countries using their peaceful nuclear programmes for military purposes is the effective application of international nuclear safeguards. The principal agency involved in this process is the International Atomic Energy Agency (IAEA). Unfortunately from the point of view of proliferation, it is technically not possible for the IAEA to detect the diversion of significant quantities of weapons-usable plutonium from safeguarded plutonium reprocessing and fuel fabrication plants.

There can be little confidence that the IAEA will be able to prevent a quantity of plutonium from becoming material unaccounted for (MUF) during the years of operation of Japanese and other countries' plutonium facilities. Former US Nuclear Regulatory Commission member, Victor Gillinsky, when testifying to the Senate Foreign Relations Committee on IAEA Safeguards, stated:

> There is no way you are going to get adequate warning when you are talking about reprocessing plants, enrichment plants or stockpiles of plutonium or highly enriched uranium. We really ought to face that.[4]

Gillinsky specifically identified the existing Tokai-mura reprocessing plant as a facility that it would not be possible to safeguard:

> I just don't think that technically the safeguard system at this plant (Tokai-mura), just on the basis of experience with safeguards systems at other plants and what we know of our own domestic safeguards system, is going to be able to detect reliably diversions of amounts of materials of significance for weapons in 1 or 2 weeks.[4]

Since there has been little real progress in safeguards effectiveness since this observation was made, Gillinsky's statement on Tokai is equally applicable to current and future plants, despite the capacity of these facilities capacity to separate far larger amounts of plutonium.

The Failure of Safeguards at Tokai-Mura

'It is difficult to measure how much plutonium there is, and that is why too much accumulation is not desirable.'[5]

A defence of Japanese and other countries' plutonium programmes is that safeguards technology has advanced since the 1970s and will continue to improve. New facilities will operate under the most advanced full-scope IAEA safeguards arrangements, including Near-Real Time Accountancy, and therefore the plutonium should not be able to be diverted for military use without detection. NRTA has been applied on a voluntary basis to the existing Tokai-mura reprocessing plant since 1978. Data collected at Tokai has been assessed by the operators, PNC, the Japan Atomic Energy Research Institute (JAERI) and the IAEA. Under the Japan Support Programme for Agency Safeguards (JASPAS) an IAEA/PNC test was conducted on the second campaign during 1985. During this test physical inventories were conducted on a weekly basis. No figures are provided as to the total volume of plutonium processed during the test. What is known is that PNC concluded, on the experience of accountancy during the test, that a diversion of greater than three kilograms would have been construed as an anomaly requiring further investigation. Our conclusion is that with two campaigns each year at the existing Tokai facility, as much as 6 kilograms of plutonium could be diverted, and no further measures would be taken, as this would be an acceptable MUF given the technical limitations of safeguards.

Japan could of course formally remove itself from the NPT (as Foreign Minister Muto suggested in 1993 – see press statement following the ASEAN regional conference) and utilize its stock of plutonium for military purposes, but the easier option would be for Japan to take advantage of the inadequacy of safeguards.

The potential for Japan to divert significant quantities of plutonium was most recently demonstrated at the Tokai-mura site in May 1994. Following accusations from the Washington-based Nuclear Control Institute, an official from PNC reluctantly admitted that 70kg of plutonium oxide had accumulated over a five-year period in the Tokai FBR Plutonium Fuel Production Facility (PFPF). The IAEA denied that the plutonium was MUF but rather 'hold-up', and remained under safeguards. The 'hold-up' consisted of plutonium dust which had gathered on exposed surfaces inside the plant.[6]

Remarkably, the Agency has stated that PNC elected to leave the material in the plant, rather than remove it. Each month PNC would declare to IAEA inspectors the amount of material involved. This would then be confirmed by the Agency, using assay methods. The only way for the Agency to verify the accuracy of PNCs and its own figures would be for the plant to be closed and cleaned out. Due to strong resistance from Japan, it was not until February 1995 that an agreement was announced with the IAEA for the clean-out of the facility to be completed in summer 1997. This should be contrasted with the statement of the IAEA General Conference in 1994, which recommended that all material be accounted for at the plant by early 1995. In addition, by giving Japan over three years to clean out its facilities, allowing the IAEA to account for most (but not all) of the plutonium, the latter is in violation of its own safeguards requirements. The timely detection goal, that is the length of time the IAEA sets itself to detect a diversion before the material can be used for military purposes, is less than three weeks for plutonium oxide. Japan, because it is Japan, is permitted to comply with IAEA safeguards when and if it so wishes.

A credible option for Japan to divert plutonium has been put forward whereby plutonium not accounted for in the Agency's hold-up figure could be concealed in low-level radioactive waste containers, which are eventually removed from the plant with inadequate inspection.[7]

The Tokai episode clearly demonstrates the discriminatory application of safeguards amongst the non-nuclear weapon states. It is unimaginable that any other non-nuclear weapon state would be permitted by the IAEA to declare that it would allow more than 70kg of weapons-usable plutonium to build-up in its facilities. As we have seen recently in the stand-off between the North Korea and the Agency, the issue of safeguards anomalies are dealt with first by the IAEA Board of Governors, and then the United Nations Security Council. The Agency and international community would rightly be unwilling to accept, for example, North Korea's declaring that it had decided to leave large quantities of weapons-usable plutonium in the Yongbyon reprocessing facility. For Japan, no such problem exists.

Even when the IAEA completes its overdue assessment, the measurement error for the IAEA safeguards equipment means that as much as 10.5 kg of the plutonium could be designated MUF, and as a result be an acceptable loss to the IAEA. For this reason the IAEA has not and cannot answer the question of how much plutonium Japan could have diverted. The measurement error for the instrument used by the IAEA in assessing the hold-up volume, has been reported at +/–15 per cent, or 10.5kg of plutonium. Consequently if up to 10kg of plutonium were to be unaccounted for, the Agency, recognizing the limitations of safeguards, would be entitled to undertake no further investigation. It was even suggested that because of the high level of contamination of the Tokai PFPF glove-boxes, the Agency's error figure was as high as 30 per cent, equivalent to 21kg of plutonium.[7] In Agency terminology 'hold-up' and 'MUF' are an acceptable consequence of plutonium reprocessing. In non-proliferation terms, however, 70kg of plutonium in this latest Tokai incident would be enough for eight nuclear weapons.

The Potential Use of Japanese Plutonium in Nuclear Weapons

> The [Japanese Defence] Agency presented various examples of
> nuclear weapons which it would be constitutionally possible to
> obtain. These included Nike-Hercules air defence missiles, and
> 155mm and 203mm howitzers.[8]

Much has been made of the non-nuclear principles of Japan, but these
are not legally binding, and as Japanese governments have made clear,
'... the possession of nuclear weapons does not contravene the Japanese
constitution', according to a statement in the Japanese Diet by Prime
Minister Nakasone in 1984.[9]

Further evidence that adds to increasing concern over Japan's commitment to nuclear weapons development was revealed in July 1994.
According to reports, the Foreign Ministry drafted a report entitled
'Prerequisites of Japan's Foreign Policy', in 1969, which recommended
that the country would maintain and where necessary develop the financial
and technical means to develop nuclear weapons – 'no matter what foreign
pressures were applied'. The report was drafted by the ministry bureau-
crats for use as a policy guideline. Further, the report recognized the need
for Japan to maintaining a policy of not possessing nuclear weapons, but
this was for the 'time being'.

The report was directly related to Japanese policy *vis-à-vis* the Treaty on
the Non-Proliferation of Nuclear Weapons (NPT), which at the time was
the subject of a major political battle inside the various Japanese
ministries. Undoubtedly, the drafting of the report was linked to reassuring
pro-nuclear weapon advocates that Japan's signature and ratification of
the Treaty would not limit its future nuclear weapon options.

Placed in the context of North-East Asia, including the Korean peninsula and the People's Republic of China, Japan's plutonium programme
can already be seen as playing a strategic role. As an advanced industrialized state with a growing surplus of weapons-usable plutonium, it is
demonstrating to countries in the region that it is not just a political and
economic power to be reckoned with, but is also a potential military
power. Contributing to the ambiguity of Japan's plutonium programme,
the inadequacy of IAEA safeguards contributes to the increasing perception that there is little that can stop Japan utilizing its plutonium for
military purposes if it so wishes.

The military potential created by Japan's plutonium programme based
around FBRs should not be underestimated. The French nuclear weapons
establishment certainly recognizes the importance of such reactors and the
plutonium they produce, 'France will be able build atomic weapons of all
kinds and within every type of range. At relatively low cost, she will be in
a position to produce large quantities of such weapons, with fast breeders
providing an abundant supply of the plutonium required.'[10] In total,

France produced between 18 and 19.5 per cent of its military inventory up to 1990 in FBRs, an amount sufficient for 400–500 nuclear warheads.

Over a ten-year operating period Japan will produce approximately 700kg of supergrade plutonium from Monju. The commercial justification for acquiring such a stockpile is that the preferred fuel for future FBRs is weapons-grade plutonium. The military justification would be that it is beyond weapons-grade in terms of quality. It gives Japan the option of having the most reliable nuclear warheads in terms of both yield and operation.

Through the use of an effective beryllium reflector, as little as 3kg of plutonium is needed for one nuclear warhead. Taking Japan's total plutonium inventory, by the year 2010 it will have sufficient excess plutonium for almost 3,000 nuclear weapons. A warhead of such a size would be suitable for an advanced cruise missile, weighing no more than 150kg, and allowing a range of around 2,500 kilometres. If Japan were to develop intercontinental ballistic missiles (ICBMs), of the multiple independently-targetable re-entry vehicle (MIRV) type, the weight would be around 350kg (Frank Barnaby, personal communication). Significantly, Japan's development of the H-2 space launch vehicle (tested in February 1994), including an Orbital Re-entry Experiment capsule, which has a payload capacity of 4000kg, would thus, if adapted for military purposes, allow more than 10 warheads for each missile.[11] Serving both an innocent and future military function is Japan's assistance to the former Soviet Union in complying with arms control agreements, including destruction of liquid fuel from its intercontinental ballistic missiles, with Japanese specialists sent to Russia during 1993.

Japan's expertise in nuclear and missile technologies would enable it to acquire a formidable nuclear weapon force if the political decision were taken to do so. The warheads would be able to be delivered with great accuracy, giving Japan the ability to target hardened military installations. Using worst-case analysis, hawkish strategists and nuclear weapons enthusiasts are likely to argue for a strategic nuclear force large enough to target many military installations in a chosen region – the so-called counterforce strategy. Such a strategy is the most destabilizing of all nuclear weapons strategies as it leads to a nuclear first-strike policy and pre-emptive strikes.

Such a development may seem far-fetched, but in a manner suggesting that a debate has already begun, former Japanese Prime Minister Miyazawa wrote in the March 1994 edition of the Japanese magazine *AERA* that, '... if the Japanese constitution would change to allow overseas military deployment ... it is likely that a decision will take place over nuclear weapons ... If nuclear weapons are not able to located on the land, then people would say, why not on submarines?'[12] Japan's Atomic Energy Research Agency Institute (JAERI) is conducting design studies on an 0.72MWt experimental deep-sea reactor (DRX) which is intended for a 'deep-sea scientific research submarine'.[13]

Conclusion

What this essay has sought to summarize is the truly awesome scale that Japan's plutonium programme is reaching. There is no evidence as yet that a decision has been made to use this material for military purposes. However, Japan's plutonium is already being used strategically both regionally and globally. The scale of the programme and the amount of material that is excess to requirements send a strong political message to the international community about Japan's capabilities. A question for the future is: will those capabilities ever be realized?

Unfortunately, fifty years after the first use of nuclear weapons, the United States and the other nuclear weapon states maintain a commitment to the deployment, targeting and ultimate use of the such weapons. One of the lessons learnt by the non-nuclear weapon states, including Japan, during the past five decades, is that nuclear weapons may or may not have a military relevance, but they undoubtedly bestow on the holder a political power that few choose to challenge. So long as the nuclear weapon states maintain their commitment to nuclear forces, the temptation for other states to take up the nuclear option will remain.

The international community must acknowledge the likelihood that at a certain point in the future factors will emerge that argue in favour of a Japanese nuclear weapons programme. We may already have reached that point, as result of the nuclear programme of North Korea, the precise status of which remains unclear. Undoubtedly, the latter is being used to argue for weaponization by Japan. More significantly in the medium to longer term is Japan's relations with the People's Republic of China.

The continuing nuclear obsession of the weapon states since 1945, and the failure of these states to meet their disarmament commitments under the NPT, send a strong, if wrong, signal to the non-nuclear world. The signal is that fifty years after their first use nuclear weapons still have an important role to play in international relations. Decision-makers in Japan through the past decades endorsed such a role for nuclear weapons, though until now they have been those belonging to the United States. Fifty years after Nagasaki, we may be close to the point where Japan's tragic relationship with nuclear weapons takes on a new and perhaps ultimately even more disastrous turn. Before it is to late, it would be appropriate at this time for Japan's decision-makers to announce a plan to reverse its plutonium and wider nuclear programmes. This unfortunately is unlikely to happen. The first fifty years of the nuclear age were devastating enough, the second could be far worse.

References

1. Gillinsky V. Plutonium, proliferation and policy. US Nuclear Regulatory Commission, Massachusetts Institute of Technology, 1 November 1976: 13. Cited in: Albright D. *Can civil plutonium be used in nuclear explosives? A*

review of statements by nuclear weapons experts. Washington DC: Federation of American Scientists, 1984.

2. *The Unlawful Alliance: Japan's supergrade plutonium and the role of the United States.* September 1994.
3. NASAP. *Nuclear Proliferation and Civilian Nuclear Power. Report of the Non-Proliferation Systems Assessment Program, Volume II: Proliferation Resistence.* Department of Energy NE – 001/2, June 1980. Cited in: Albright D: 22.
4. Gillinsky V. Statement to Hearings before the Senate Foreign Relations Committee on IAEA programs of safeguards, 97th Congress, 1st session, 43, 1981. Cited in: Greenberg EVC. *The NPT and Plutonium.* Presentation to 1993 Preparatory Committee meeting of parties to the Treaty on the Non-Proliferation of Nuclear Weapons. Washington DC: Nuclear Control Institute, 1993.
5. Nakano H. Japan to retrieve lost plutonium in fuel plant. *Shinichi Kishima,* Tokyo, 10 May 1994.
6. International Atomic Energy Agency. Statement PR 94/23, 25 May 1994.
7. Citizen's Coalition Against the Plutonium Fast Breeder Program. *PNC's Tokai Plutonium Fuel Production Facility's 70 Kilogram Plutonium Discrepancy.* Kyoto: CCAPFBP, 1994.
8. Japanese Defence Agency White Paper. *Asahi Shimbun,* 15 October 1980.
9. Nakasone Y. Reported in *Krasnaya Zvezda,* 18 March 1984.
10. Thiry J. Reported in: *The Impact of a Power Station on Gwynedd.* Gwynedd County Council, 1976.
11. *Space News,* 22 March 1993.
12. *Itar-Tass,* Moscow, 3 March 1993.
13. Nuclear Services Section, Australian Nuclear Science and Technology Organisation. *Nuclear Developments in the Asia and Pacific Region.* Canberra: Department of External Affairs, 1993: 23.

(24 May 1995)

Shaun Burnie is Research Coordinator for Greenpeace International, based in Amsterdam. He holds a Master's degree in War Studies from King's College, University of London. At Greenpeace he specialises in the proliferation problems of commercial nuclear programmes, with particular focus on North-East Asia. He has worked and travelled in Japan and the Korean peninsula. He writes in a personal capacity and the chapter does not necessarily reflect the views of Greenpeace International.

Correspondence: Greenpeace International, Keizersgracht 176, 1016 DW Amsterdam, The Netherlands.

Current Attitudes to the Atomic Bombings in Japan

KAZUYO YAMANE

There are conspicuous differences in current attitudes toward the atomic bombing between the Japanese government and the Japanese people. The Japanese government has still not admitted war responsibility fifty years after the end of the Second World War. Former Prime Minister Hosokawa apologized to Asian countries for the damage done by Japan during the war for the first time in 1993, but refused to make any offers of compensation. Twenty million Asians died during the war. An estimated 200,000 women from Korea, the Philippines and other nations were forced to work as sex slaves for Japanese soldiers. The Japanese government has continually evaded the question of state responsibility for aggression. This attitude is related to the government's refusal to admit war responsibility to atomic bomb victims in the *Hibakusha* Aid Law. The current attitudes of the Japanese government have been criticized not only by the Japanese people but also by other Asians.

The World Court Project

When Japan was asked for an opinion on the legality of the use of nuclear weapons by the International Court of Justice in 1994, the Japanese government responded that it is not against International Law to use nuclear weapons. This was severely criticized by both the atomic bomb survivors and the rest of the Japanese people: the government subsequently withdrew this response. Japan should have issued a report on the consequences of the atomic bombings and become a leader in the movement to make nuclear weapons illegal. Japan, however, abstained in a vote which asked the International Court of Justice for an advisory opinion on the question: 'Is the threat or use of nuclear weapons in any circumstance permitted under international law?' in the United Nations General Assembly on 19 November 1994. The resolution was sponsored by the Non-Aligned Movement and supported by a majority of states. The attitude of the Japanese government was criticized by many because Japan is the only country that has experienced the use of nuclear weapons. The World Court Project making nuclear weapons illegal is supported by many people in Japan.

The Smithsonian Exhibition

The Japanese government also took an ambiguous position on the Smithsonian Institution issue. The Smithsonian Institution's National Air and Space Museum in Washington planned to mark the 50th anniversary of the dropping of the first atomic bomb with an exhibit entitled 'The Last Act: The Atomic Bomb and the End of World War II' in May 1995. The aim of the exhibition was to describe the outbreak and development of the Second World War and to look at nuclear weapons from the perspective of the Cold War. Artifacts and photographs from peace museums in Hiroshima and Nagasaki were to be included in the first exhibit on the use of atomic weapons in Japan to be held at a US national museum. Ultimately, however, the Smithsonian Institution revised the exhibit, excluding photographs and belongings of atomic bomb victims, because of growing pressure from Congress and Second World War veterans. The modified display, according to Smithsonian Secretary Michael Heyman, will consist only of *Enola Gay*, the B-29 bomber that dropped the first atomic bomb, together with information about the aeroplane and a video about the crew. The Smithsonian Institution had proposed a broad review of history, including the argument that the use of atomic bombs was meant as a display of power to the Soviet Union rather than as a military measure to hasten the end of the war. Veterans' groups, in response, claimed that the use of the atomic bomb was justified, insisting that it had shortened the war and made an invasion of Japan unnecessary, thereby saving the lives of between 500,000 and one million US soldiers.

When the Smithsonian Institution announced its decision not to include information on the casualties and damage inflicted on Japan, Foreign Minister Yohei Kono said: 'The government is not in a position to comment on the decision by the Smithsonian Institution.'[1] On the other hand, Hiroshima Mayor Takashi Hiraoka responded: 'It is extremely regrettable. Thinking of our wish to strengthen US public opinion favouring a non-nuclear world, our disappointment becomes stronger.' Hiroshi Harada, director of the Hiroshima Peace Memorial Museum, remarked that 'It is very deplorable. I'd like to think of an independent exhibition on atomic bomb victims in the United States.' Barton J. Bernstein, Professor of History at Stanford University in California, who served as an adviser for the exhibition and protested at frequent changes in the exhibition plans, said: 'The result can only encourage ignorance, not substantial understanding. That is the unstated purpose of the newly revised *Enola Gay* exhibit in Washington, D.C.'[2] He added: 'Perhaps various media events planned in the United States for mid-1995 re-examining critically the decision and meaning of the use of the atomic bomb may help to spur analysis, promote understanding, and nurture lament and regret.' Nagasaki Mayor Hitoshi Motoshima held the same view:

I am distressed that the United States, where freedom of speech is an important right, would make such a move. [However], it's good that the dispute over the show helped raise concerns over the atomic bombings. We plan to continue pointing out the horrors of the atomic bombings.[3]

Although the Japanese government failed to protest against the decision of the Smithsonian Institution, Japanese peace groups are planning to hold an exhibition on the aftermath of the atomic bombings on Hiroshima and Nagasaki in the United States. It is encouraging to know, according to Professor Bernstein, that 'many Americans are willing to look critically at their own past.' A new American group called 'The 1995 Disarmament Coalition: 50 Years Too Many – Disarm Now!' hopes to organize an alternative exhibit on the sidewalk in front of the Smithsonian Institution's museum, featuring photographs of the victims of Hiroshima and Nagasaki.

The Smithsonian Institution's drastic revision of the original exhibit deprived visitors of their right to know. Varying views of history should have been presented so that visitors would have been able to decide what really happened in Hiroshima and Nagasaki and consider the implications for the past, present and future.

The United States also planned to issue a controversial stamp in 1995 commemorating the use of the atomic bomb. The stamp's design showed a mushroom cloud with the caption, 'Atomic bombs hasten war's end, August 1945.' Responding to criticism from Japan, the United States cancelled this plan in December 1994. The Japan Confederation of Atomic and Hydrogen Bomb Victims Organizations also called for the US Postal Service to recall the stamp, stating:

> The planned stamp is an insult ... to hundreds of thousands of people who were thrown into the hell created by the two A-bombs while they were still alive, and were miserably killed like insects ... the U.S. government should admit that its atomic attacks on Hiroshima and Nagasaki were atrocious acts violating international law and apologize ... the United States should launch an effort for the total elimination of nuclear weapons, beginning with the renunciation of its own nuclear arsenal.[4]

Since the United States was able to scrap plans to issue an atomic-bomb stamp, it might also be possible for the Smithsonian Institute to reconsider its decision to revise the *Enola Gay* exhibit. Unfortunately, a US publishing firm reacted by issuing a look-alike mushroom-cloud-like seal that accuses the US government of surrendering to Japan. The company stated that it would donate part of the revenue from the sale of the stamps to groups that are helping atomic bomb victims.[5] Considering the feelings of the atomic bomb survivors, it is insensitive for the company to attempt to make money by taking advantage of the stamp issue.

The Smithsonian Institution situation mirrors that of a national peace museum for Japan. Construction was originally planned for 1995, but has since been delayed. The first plan for the War Dead Peace Memorial Hall was to exhibit artifacts glorifying the aggresive nature of war. This plan was strongly criticized by local residents, historians, war victims from other Asian countries, pacifist groups, and others. Their reaction arose because the original conception of the museum exhibits included no mention of Japanese aggression in the Second World War. The government had at first promised to include information on Japanese aggression in the museum, but later reversed its position. In an unprecedented act, the historians serving on the museum steering committee resigned *en masse*, forcing the government to reconsider the plans. The Japanese government wishes to avoid exhibiting information on Japanese aggression in the Second World War because it does not want to admit any responsibility for the war.

Rumiko Nishino, an author of books on the biological experiments of Unit 731 and the use of non-Japanese women as sex slaves, criticized the plan for a national peace museum, saying that the construction cost of 12.3 billion yen (about £ 77 million) should be used to compensate Asian victims of Japanese aggression during the Second World War. These victims are, in fact, not only Asians, but also include former prisoners of war and ex-civilian internees from four countries (Britain, the United States, Australia and New Zealand) who are seeking a formal written apology and compensation for their suffering at the hands of Japanese soldiers during the Second World War. The Japanese government insists that the compensation issue has been resolved under international law, citing compensation at the state level between Japan and other countries, and the waiver of other compensation claims. Martyn Day, a lawyer, reported that, 'Germany spent 100 times more than Japan in individual compensation. Japan has spent 1.5 trillion yen annually for its war veterans and their relatives.'[6]

The Non-Proliferation Treaty

What is the attitude of the Japanese government towards the Non-Proliferation Treaty? In November 1994 the UN General Assembly First Committee adopted a resolution submitted by Japan on the ultimate elimination of nuclear weapons. The resolution states that the UN should urge non-signatory nations to join the NPT at the earliest opportunity. Japan supports the proposal of countries currently possessing nuclear arms that the NPT be indefinitely extended. This position has been criticized by the Japanese people because of its discriminatory provision in favour of countries that belong to the 'Nuclear Club'. Non-nuclear signatories are not only prohibited from making or possessing nuclear arms, but must undergo periodic inspections by the International Atomic Energy Agency.

The nations with nuclear arsenals, on the contrary, are exempt from such prohibitions and inspections. As the non-aligned countries point out, indefinite extension of the NPT will preserve the *status quo* of the five states that have declared themselves nuclear powers. Japanese peace groups insist that the issue is not to preserve the *status quo* by calling only for the ultimate elimination of nuclear weapons, but their immediate abolition.

Plutonium

Another issue is Japan's use of nuclear power in its energy programme. Some countries are suspicious that plutonium might be used for Japanese production of nuclear weapons because Japan is eager to reprocess nuclear fuel and to develop fast breeder reactors to produce more plutonium. The Science and Technology Agency informed the Diet how much plutonium was stockpiled in Japan for the first time in the autumn of 1993, in order to dispel any suspicion of its use for weapons manufacture. According to its 1994 White Paper on Atomic Energy, the agency disclosed that 4,684 kilograms of plutonium are presently stockpiled in Japan, while 6,197 kilograms of plutonium are held by British and French agencies which are reprocessing spent fuel for Japanese electric power companies. The Japanese government insists that it has no intention of putting plutonium to military use. Professor Tokunosuke Nakajima of Chuo University insisted on the following steps:

> First, there should be no more plutonium than we have so far pro-
> duced, either for military or for commercial use. It is important to
> note that nuclear power plants should be advised not to 'separate'
> the plutonium that is inevitably produced as long as they are in
> operation. Second, the Japanese government should discontinue the
> policy of reprocessing all spent fuel from nuclear power plants.
> Thirdly, France and Britain should be told to stop offering their
> reprocessing services and Japan should begin negotiations for ending
> its contracts with them. If these policies are carried out, Japan will be
> forced to question its present policy of building more nuclear power
> plants and consider a phasing out, instead of a reckless building, of
> light water reactors.[7]

After the great Hanshin earthquake in January 1995 left more than 5,000 people dead and nearly 300,000 homeless, Science and Technology Agency Director-General Makiko Tanaka promised to reconsider safety standards for nuclear power plants. In a related incident, opponents of a planned nuclear power plant in Niigata Prefecture overwhelmingly won a referendum held on 7 February of this year. The Japanese people are suspicious of the safety of nuclear power plants: a gap exists in the attitudes of the public and the government in respect to the plutonium issue.

The Revival of Japanese Militarism

The issues of the Smithsonian exhibition and the national peace museum in Japan are related to current political conditions in the United States and Japan. The justification of the atomic bombings in the Smithsonian exhibition is related to the US policy to maintain its superiority in nuclear weapons through the NPT. The national peace museum issue shows the Japanese government's stubbornness in not recognizing Japan's aggressive role in the Second World War. This is directly connected to the revival of Japanese militarism as part of US military strategy. According to the US Security Strategy for the East Asia Pacific Region, the United States alliance with Japan is 'the linchpin of US security policy in Asia'.[8] The US–Japan Security Treaty is a military alliance under which Japan is subordinate to the United States. The ambiguous attitude of the Japanese government to the atomic bombs stems from this situation: while it appeared superficially to listen to the voice of the Japanese people, it in fact followed another policy in maintaining the US–Japan Security Treaty. This explains why there are large gaps between the government and the Japanese people over the World Court Project, the Smithsonian exhibition, the NPT and plutonium. Nevertheless, however conservative the Japanese government may be, the peace movement in Japan continues to work to change the situation.

Current Efforts for Peace in Japan

Japanese peace groups are eager for change from the present situation because there has been no alteration in domestic or foreign policy despite political leadership passing from the Liberal Democratic Party to the Social Democratic Party, with a new Prime Minister. The Japan–US military alliance has been expanded to cover the whole world, and US bases in Japan have been strengthened as part of US nuclear strategy. The World Conference against Atomic and Hydrogen Bombs, held every summer since 1955, is now the key rallying point for the promotion of international actions for a nuclear-weapon-free peace. The Appeal from Hiroshima and Nagasaki for a Total Ban and Elimination of Nuclear Weapons has spread to more than 160 countries. This campaign was started by anti-nuclear peace groups in 1985: about 100 million signatures have been collected world-wide, with over 46 million signatures coming from Japan, by the end of 1994. This greatly influenced the UN resolution on the legality of nuclear weapons on 19 November 1994 and the World Court Project.

In Japan, more than 50 per cent of local municipalities, representing about 70 per cent of the total Japanese population, have declared themselves nuclear-free zones. Local assemblies are adopting resolutions demanding an international treaty for the elimination of nuclear weapons.

In order to make public the damage and consequences of the use of nuclear weapons in Hiroshima and Nagasaki and rally opinion for the abolition of nuclear weapons, Japanese peace groups are planning to send information panels and videos about the atomic bombings overseas. A peace march for the abolition of nuclear weapons is planned from 5 May to 6 August, both in Japan and other countries. An international symposium against nuclear weapons will be held in Hiroshima from 31 July to 2 August by the Disarmament Special Committee of NGOs. The 1995 World Conference against Atomic and Hydrogen Bombs will be held from 6 to 9 August in Hiroshima and Nagasaki, preceded by an international conference from 3 to 5 August in Hiroshima. It should be noted that both survivors of the atomic bombs and victims of nuclear tests will attend the conference, including those of US nuclear tests in the Marshall Islands and of a Soviet nuclear test at Semipalatinsk in Kazakhstan. Information on these and similar events is published in the *International Peace Bureau News*.

The events in Hiroshima and Nagasaki are less well known throughout the world than they should be. It is very important to provide information on the aftermath of these atomic bombings, as they mark the beginning of the nuclear age. Although many materials on the aftermath are available in Japanese, few are in English. The following materials have been translated into English and provide information on what really happened in Hiroshima and Nagasaki.

- *Hiroshima–Nagasaki: A Pictorial Record of the Atomic Destruction* was made possible by a citizens' movement in 1977–78. Valuable photographs taken immediately after the atomic bombing are reproduced. The photographs are also available in an easily accessible pamphlet, '*Days to Remember: An Account of the Bombings of Hiroshima and Nagasaki*'.[9]
- A display, *Atomic Bombs – a Documentary of Hiroshima and Nagasaki*, consists of thirty A2 size panels. These can be used in peace museums, schools, conferences, and so forth, to show the aftermath of Hiroshima and Nagasaki. The photographs were taken by both Japanese and American photographers immediately after the atomic bombings.*
- The Hiroshima and Nagasaki issue marks only the beginning of the nuclear age. The number of radiation victims has been steadily increasing ever since. *Exposure: Victims of Radiation Speak Out* describes various victims of radiation in nuclear tests, accidents in nuclear power plants, the nuclear fuel cycle from the mining of nuclear resources through the reprocessing of spent fuel, the disposal of radioactive waste, and nuclear weapons factories. It also follows the increase in the number of radiation victims since 1945.[10]

* Hiroshima-Nagasaki Publishing Committee, *Atomic Bombs: A Documentary of Hiroshima and Nagasaki*. Tokyo: The Association for Creating Peace Museums.

- *Free our Planet of Nuclear Weapons: Our Town, Ocean and Motherland* is a 55-minute video produced by the Organizing Committee of the World Conference against the Atomic and Hydrogen Bombs to mark the 50th anniversary of the atomic bombings of Hiroshima and Nagasaki. The video tells of the terrible human costs of the nuclear arms race. An English edition is available: Japanese grassroots anti-nuclear groups will send it as a free gift to any peace group overseas which requests one.[†]
- *On a Paper Crane* is an animated film for peace. It shows a girl named Sadako who died because of a radiation-related disease and is an extremely useful tool for informing children about Hiroshima.[‡]

In order to work for the total elimination of nuclear weapons, it is never too late to disseminate information on the aftermath of the atomic bombing of Hiroshima and Nagasaki. We live in a nuclear age, and the dangers of nuclear war have not gone away. It is encouraging to know that there are many peace groups working wholeheartedly for peace throughout the world. Their efforts are often ignored by the mass media: it is essential to exchange information and opinions at grassroots level. Hiroshima and Nagasaki mark the beginning of the nuclear age: through our efforts for peace, we hope to end the present nuclear age and consign it to history.

Acknowledgements

I should like to thank for their help Craig Delaney, Peter van den Dungen, Richard Falk, Robert Green, Shigeo Nishimori and my husband, Kyunosuke Yamane.

References

1. *Enola Gay* display shell of former self. *The Japan Times*, 1 February 1995.
2. Bernstein B. The Smithsonian 'sells out' over *Enola Gay*. *The Daily Yomiuri*, 2 February 1995.
3. Gingrich: A-bomb exhibit due for overhaul. *The Daily Yomiuri*, 29 January 1995.
4. A-bomb survivors protest to US about stamp. *The Daily Yomiuri*, 9 December 1994.
5. A-bomb stamp look-alikes on market. *The Daily Yomiuri*, 23 December 1994.
6. Allied ex-prisoners seek redress in Tokyo. *The Daily Yomiuri*, 1 February 1995.
7. Nakajima T. Japanese plutonium recycling policy in relation to the elimination of nuclear weapons. Presentation to the 1994 World Conference against Atomic and Hydrogen Bombs International Meeting, Hiroshima, August 1994.

[†] Available from World Conference against Atomic & Hydrogen Bombs, 6–19–23 Shinbashi, Minato-ku, Tokyo 105, Japan. Fax: 81–3–3431–8781.
[‡] Peace Animation Association, *On a Paper Crane*, Tokyo: Peace Animation Association, Taiyoh-biru 7F, 3–16–2 Shinbashi Minatoku, Tokyo 105.

8. US affirms commitment to a Pacific defense. *The Daily Yomiuri*, 28 February 1995.
9. Hiroshima-Nagasaki Publishing Committee. *Days to Remember: An Account of the Bombing of Hiroshima and Nagasaki*. Tokyo: 1981: 36.
10. The *Chagoju* newspaper, *Exposure: Victims of Radiation Speak Out*. Tokyo, New York, London: Kodansha International, 1992.

(20 March 1995)

Correspondence: Grassroots House, 9–11 Masugata, Kochi City 780, Japan.

Illegal Trafficking in Nuclear Fissile Materials: Likely Customers and Suppliers

JASJIT SINGH

Illegal trafficking in nuclear materials and technology has been going on for a long time and has been the primary source of the clandestine nuclear weapon programmes of states like Iraq, Pakistan and North Korea. The illegality has essentially been in relation to existing national laws of states. These laws have evolved over a period of time, generally to regulate the export of materials and technology leading to nuclear proliferation. Some states have also adopted *ad hoc* arrangements by forming cartels like the Nuclear Suppliers Group. The Treaty for the Non-proliferation of Nuclear Weapons (NPT) provides the legal framework for applying rules governing the flow of nuclear materials to non-nuclear weapon states who are party to the treaty. Transfers of materials and even weapons have been taking place under the provisions of the NPT to states party to the NPT who are acknowledged weapon states (like the United Kingdom) and non-weapon states (such as Germany and South Korea until recently). But the issue has assumed new and critical dimensions in recent years. At one level, the advanced status and extent of the nuclear weapon programmes of Pakistan and Iraq highlighted the scope and implications of illegal transfers. The focus has certainly been more intense on Iraq, since it had obligations to remain a non-nuclear weapon state under the NPT to which it was a signatory (not to mention its invasion and occupation of Kuwait). The primary source of Iraq's nuclear materials and technology was the advanced industrialized states party to the NPT.

The second development has been the disintegration of the Soviet Union, which held the largest stock of nuclear weapons and material in the world. In 1986 the Soviet Union possessed 45,000 nuclear warheads (15,000 more than their Western estimates). Its stockpile of weapon-grade material (including warheads) was believed to exceed 1,200 tons in 1993.[1] The break-up of the Soviet Union into fifteen republics split the nuclear arsenals, installations and stockpiles; and the continuing socio-economic crisis in the former Soviet territories has raised serious concerns about increased traffic in nuclear materials, besides the flow of technological mercenaries. At the same time, the altered international political architecture has created new dimensions in international security which appear to drive nuclear proliferation incentives. Many questions related to the issue of illegal trafficking, therefore, need to be addressed.

Illegal Fissile Materials

The basic concern about trafficking in nuclear materials is that of hori-
zontal weapons proliferation. While the scope of what might constitute
nuclear materials in this context has been significantly widened in recent
years (by including dual-use items by many states), the fact is that the
International Atomic Energy Agency (IAEA) has clearly defined what items
are included in the definition of nuclear materials that are brought under
the IAEA safeguard system. Special 'fissionable' materials are defined in
Article XX of the IAEA Statute, and include 'plutonium-239; uranium-
233; uranium enriched in isotopes 235 or 233; any material containing
one or more of the foregoing ...'; and 'source' material is defined to
include 'uranium containing the mixture of isotopes occurring in nature;
uranium depleted in the isotope 235; thorium; any of the foregoing in
the form of metal, alloy, chemical compound, or concentrate.'[2] Other
material may be added to the list by the IAEA Board of Governors. But
this authority has never been exercised, no doubt because the list of fissile
material remains complete and comprehensive.

Smuggling of Fissile Material

Reports about the smuggling of fissile material shot into prominence in
1994, and it appears that the international community is no longer in a
position to be certain about the whereabouts of fissile material necessary
for making nuclear weapons. The fact that the 'material unaccounted for'
could run into very large quantities is an additional concern. The
'significant quantities' limit to such material now appears to be on the
high side and nuclear bombs can be made with lower quantities of fissile
material than previously thought. A report of the Natural Resources
Defense Council in 1994 asked for the threshold of danger to be lowered
(from the present 8 kilogram limit to as little as 1 kilogram of plutonium).[3]
Richard Garwin endorses the idea of revising the limits which have come
to make the distinction between what is legally accounted for or not. If
this is so, the dangers inherent in the making and stockpiling of nuclear
weapons and the risks associated with illegal transfers of even small
quantities of fissile material may be much higher than the world has
believed so far.

The smuggling of fissile material became an issue after cases were
recorded in Germany. The record of actual or suspected cases of illegal
transfer of radioactive and fissile material to Germany was as follows:

Year	Incidents
1990	4
1991	41
1992	158
1993	241
1994	90 (first six months)

More than one-third of these 534 incidents resulted from questionable evidence, and mostly involved misreporting, or attempted deception including sting operations. Out of all these, material was seized in only 46 cases, with fissile material being involved in 15 of them. Three cases involved weapons-grade material. In addition there were a number of cases of very small amounts (milligrams) of plutonium from smoke- and chemical weapon-detectors. The total amount of material seized in Germany amounts to 11.4 kilograms of natural uranium, 3.3 kilograms of low-enriched uranium, 0.8 grams of highly-enriched uranium, and 408.4 grams of plutonium. The most serious discovery in Germany, in August 1994, was believed to be part of a $250 million deal to smuggle 4 kilograms.[4] Concerns heightened when authorities were faced with claims that up to 150 kilograms of plutonium might have been transferred from Russia and stored in Switzerland. The head of German intelligence, Bernd Schmidbauer, claimed that 'The material which was found in Germany is only a portion – the tip of the iceberg', and went on to assert that 'Europe-wide, there are about 300 cases of such materials ... the smallest part of it showing up in Germany'. The German Foreign Minister, Klaus Kinkel, asserted that 'the false impression is being created that this is a (German) problem ... There are similar problems in France, in Switzerland, and in other European countries'.[5] In December 1994 three kilograms of highly enriched uranium were seized by Czech authorities.[6] There were reports that nearly 400 kilograms of weapon-grade uranium had been confiscated in the Black Sea port of Odessa (Ukraine) by security police in December 1993.

It is clear that while individual seizures do not indicate anything more than a 'trickle', the very fact they are taking place is a cause for serious concern, especially when no clear assessment can be made of what is not being intercepted. What we do not know, we do not know.

Likely Customers

The likely end-customers for fissile materials fall into two broad categories: states and non-state actors. This would not include what may be termed transitional customers – those who are buying with a view to sell. As regards the states, customer states would have to fulfil two fundamental criteria. Firstly, they would not have access to fissile material through legal processes; and secondly, they would perceive the acquisition of such material as imperative.

The five nuclear weapon states require fissile material for their nuclear warheads, and have acquired it in large quantities. But the present international regime has legitimized their nuclear weapons through the NPT; and any procurement of fissile material by these states would not constitute an illegal activity in terms of existing norms. At the same time there are a large number of states with a highly developed and extensive base of nuclear science and technology. More than thirty states design, build and operate nuclear power and research reactors in their own right. They have the capability to manufacture their own fissile material if required. Obviously such countries are not in the market for illegal acquisitions. The notable examples include Belgium, Canada, Germany, India, Japan, Sweden, Switzerland, to name a few. Countries which have structured their power programmes around the use of plutonium, like Japan and India, would have fissile material available within the country as part of peaceful programmes. However, reactor plutonium is not very useful for bomb making.

On the other hand, the overwhelming majority of the developing and many developed countries do not have a well-established nuclear science and technology base, and some of them have been operating small research reactors or a handful of power reactors established with foreign assistance. In almost all cases international safeguards apply – most of these countries are members of the NPT and subject to a comprehensive safeguards regime. Theoretically, any or all these states could acquire fissile material illegally. The acquisition of fissile material alone is not enough to make the bomb – it is also necessary to have the know-how and associated technology to convert the fissile material into a usable weapon. The states that might actually seek to acquire fissile material illegally would also be in search of corresponding technologies and equipment for bomb-making. Their behaviour would be guided by the second factor – *the motivation to possess fissile material for making nuclear weapons*.

It is thus possible to shorten the list of potential customers considerably. In some cases there has been substantive circumstantial evidence of clandestine nuclear weapon programmes – the cases of Iraq and Pakistan stand out among them. *Iraq*'s scope for illegal acquisition has been reduced following the Gulf War and consequent steps to eliminate its nuclear programme under UN authority. But because opportunities and access to fissile material have increased since the Gulf War (primarily due to the disintegration of the Soviet Union), Iraq may look to the black market for material. If it wanted to re-establish its nuclear weapon programme, the only way it could do so would be to acquire adequate stocks of fissile material.

Pakistan started its nuclear weapon programme in January 1972. It had followed the plutonium route initially, which was thwarted when France backed off in midstream in 1976 from building the contracted reprocessing plant. However, important technological information was already in Pakistan's hands, and it also managed to keep the New Labs reprocessing facility and the larger one at Chashma outside the IAEA inspection regime. Meanwhile Pakistan pursued the second track of obtaining fissile material through a uranium enrichment process. There is a consensus in Pakistan that it must sustain its nuclear weapon capability at any cost and there is substantial evidence that it has obtained nuclear technology, components and materials from the United States, China and West European countries. Each disclosure led to new laws being instituted in the United States; but Pakistan managed to acquire a nuclear capability by 1987, mainly because the United States was not willing to enforce its own laws owing to Cold War dynamics and the Soviet invasion of Afghanistan.

Pakistan, however, did not abandon the second track of a plutonium route. Its nuclear science and technology base remains extremely narrow in spite of two and half decades of a weapons programme. It has not added a single MW of nuclear energy in more than two decades after it acquired a 125 MWe power reactor from Canada. Pakistan's stockpile of highly-enriched uranium will remain small, especially when the treaty to prohibit production of fissile material now being negotiated comes into force. Meanwhile, it would appear to be a prime candidate to increase the stockpile of weapon-grade uranium and also acquire plutonium to expand its weapons option for future.

Iran is generally believed to be working towards a weapons programme. Bordered by a nuclear-armed Pakistan on one side and Iraq with its weapons programme on the other, Iran has strong incentives to acquire a weapons capability. US official sources have been quoted as saying that Iran could be as little as five years away from making the bomb. Iran is party to the NPT, and its facilities are under safeguards. The IAEA has found no evidence to suggest that Iran is using those facilities for a weapons programme. If Iran is to move towards a nuclear weapons capability, acquiring fissile material through illicit means could be an attractive option. The situation in the territories of the former Soviet Union, the high incidence of smuggling through Central Asia, and the poor conditions of nuclear materials control and safety in Russia could provide the opportunities to do so.

The other countries generally reported to be interested in a nuclear weapons programme, but unable to acquire fissile material legally, include Libya and Algeria. Saudi Arabia has also reputedly sought to acquire nuclear weapons, mainly by funding the efforts of other countries like Iraq; and its support to Pakistan's programme is well known. However, with growing uncertainties as to the future evolution of international political and strategic architecture, the nuclear market could flourish rather than decline unless appropriate early steps are taken.

The second category of customer would be the *non-state actors*. While identifying states as customers is a difficult process, the difficulties, variables and uncertainties of focusing on non-state actors are monumental. Likely customers may be identified by examining their motives. Nuclear weapons have really been instruments of politics although their political impact derives from their military application. Although nuclear weapons have been used only in Hiroshima and Nagasaki, during the past 50 years there have been over 49 incidents involving threatened use. In every case the target country either did not possess nuclear weapons or was usable to respond in kind. In the hands of non-state actors fissile materials conjure up apocalyptic scenarios of nuclear terrorism. On the other hand, conventional terrorism is a much easier and accessible tool, and terrorist groups may not find greater advantages in nuclear terrorism. But this line of argument may be missing the point altogether: that fissile materials, and possible nuclear warheads, could become a powerful political tool for coercing a particular state or the international community at large. The fact that such action would be extremely difficult, if not impossible, to prevent or counter raises the stakes considerably. Clearly, the acquisition by non-state actors of fissile materials, let alone nuclear weapons, is a serious problem, but in view of the trends it may not be insurmountable. The probability of non-state actors acquiring such capabilities are extremely low; but were they able to do so (possibly helped by radical governments on ideological grounds), the impact on international peace, security and stability would be grave.

Likely Sources

The likely sources of black market fissile material fall in two categories. Firstly, there are those states whose control over fissile materials and their physical security has been less than adequate. Secondly, states may be willing to supply fissile materials for ideological reasons or if they perceive strategic advantages in doing so. After all, the United States has provided the lion's share of the United Kingdom's nuclear arsenal, except that the various transactions were within the national laws and in consonance with the international trends of the Cold War. On the other hand, China has been suspected of assisting Pakistan in the design of a nuclear weapon in the early 1980s. In a world where alliance systems are eroding, it is conceivable that states may transfer fissile material to other states (and, less likely, to non-state actors) on ideological and/or strategic grounds.

But the bigger problem arises from the first contingency. These unplanned and uncontrolled transfers could take place because of poor physical security of nuclear installations and materials, exploitation of loop-holes and errors in the accounting of nuclear material due to the scale of material involved, or even due to criminal activity by insiders for profit or other motives, in conjunction or otherwise with outsiders. It needs to be noted that *most of the weapon-usable materials in the world are not governed by any international safeguards.* All the known and suspected incidents of illegal trafficking in nuclear materials have occurred from a nuclear weapon state party to the NPT.

The current security systems of many states are deficient. The Convention on Physical Protection of Nuclear Materials, concluded in 1980, does not have verification procedures to ensure its implementation. The statistical margin of error in material accounting could be much higher, since such accounting is of little utility in civil facilities where weapon-grade material is flowing through the production process as powder, gas, or liquid, and not useful for accurate accounting purposes. At the same time, the civilian fuel cycles of the United States, Russia and China are only partially covered by IAEA, while those of France and the United Kingdom are under EURATOM rather than IAEA control. The biggest source of fissile material, the military fuel cycles of nuclear weapon states, are totally excluded from any external overview or transparency.

There is little doubt that the security measures in the nuclear facilities of the former Soviet Union are inadequate – the deficiencies have been acknowledged by Russian experts.[8] Approximately 1,000 tons of weapon-usable highly-enriched uranium (HEU) and 170 tons of separated plutonium in weapons or available for weapons, and 30 tons of separated civil plutonium are stored in Russia under inadequate conditions of physical security and of material control and accounting. Russian President Boris Yeltsin has said that 40 per cent of individual private businessmen and 60 per cent of all Russian companies have been corrupted by organized crime. Corruption has spread to the Russian military. In 1992 nearly 40,000 charges of corruption were brought against Russian military personnel; and the Russian defence ministry reported 4,000 cases of conventional weapons missing from military depots in 1992, with the figure rising to nearly 6,500 cases in 1993.[9] According to a 1993 US Department of Energy report, nearly 3,000 officers have been disciplined for engaging in questionable business practices, and 46 generals and other officers await trial on criminal charges.[10]

A major source of income for criminal organizations in Russia is the illegal export of strategic materials. It is also generally agreed that the Soviet/Russian system of nuclear safeguards had been based on the 'human element', with the KGB and the military playing the key roles. According to experts, 'The economic, political and social crisis in society has eroded this foundation and clarified the inadequacy of the current technical and organisational procedures to safeguard nuclear materials.'[11] Inherent technical detection difficulties in the former Soviet Union are compounded by the lack of trained personnel and detection equipment, and the borders have become extremely porous. While seeking to improve the technical controls and safeguards, Russian Ministry of Atomic Energy (MINATOM) officials acknowledge the deficiencies. Dr AV Izmailov of MINATOM lists

the following factors which need to be taken into account in bringing
about improvements:[12]

- Rising crime.
- The need for tighter security in actual operations. For example,
  when originally conceived, security systems did not account for the
  activities of unauthorized persons from within or outside, the main
  threat now.
- Russian nuclear security systems require more personnel than
  those of the West.
- A lack of official regulation of nuclear safeguards.

The United States has come forward with the Nunn–Lugar plan to help
Russia tighten its control over nuclear materials. Recent assessments indi-
cate that this plan, launched three years ago, has 'failed to date to improve
MPC&A [fissile material protection, control and accounting] in Russia'.[13]

There is a need to ensure that attention is not diverted from other
possible sources because of the high risk of illegal flow of fissile material
from the former Soviet Union. Theoretically, this risk exists in all states
engaged in the production of fissile material in any form. But once
again, the extent of control and protection would be the regulating factor.
There is also a risk that states themselves may assist in transferring fissile
materials for ideological and/or strategic considerations.

The Networks

Identifying the potential buyers and suppliers will remain a matter of
deductive logic, and specific evidence, if it emerges, will be more a unique
occurrence rather than an indication of a pattern. An assessment of the
networks, therefore, of necessity, will remain even more difficult. In all
probability, the network is likely to be established as a temporary solution
to the perceived needs and to be tailor-made for the purpose.

Since the most likely buyer of black market fissile material would be a
state, the network would be set up by the intelligence agencies of the state
concerned. They would probably be assisted by organized mafia and
criminal gangs as field operators to supplement their own agents. Russian
mafias are even more notorious than their traditional European counter-
parts, and the Chinese triads have been increasingly active in recent years.
The important point is that the existence, operation and success of a network may never be known.

However, some clues may be forthcoming from operations involving the
management of the large sums of money which would inevitably be
involved in fissile material transactions. There is already an extensive network for drug money laundering in the world. Drug traffic from the
Golden Crescent (Pakistan–Afghanistan–Iran) is generally estimated to be
worth $10 billion a year. It may be recalled that Mehran Bank in Pakistan

was deeply involved in drug money laundering: even the Army Chief received at least $3 billion from the bank, which he claimed had been transferred to the intelligence agencies.[14] Other banks have been known to carry out clandestine and criminal activities, including larger scale drug money laundering; of these, the case of the BCCI (Bank of Credit and Commerce International) stands out in recent times.

The Way Ahead

The potential and actual risks of illegal trafficking in nuclear materials needs to be addressed by the international community with the highest priority. The greatest danger, of course, would be if nuclear warheads were diverted. There have been unconfirmed reports of such diversion. Tactical weapons are directly usable and are thus the most susceptible to illegal transfer. The vulnerability of weapons increases during transportation. In the Soviet Union, thousands of warheads were believed to be regularly transported every year in the process of warhead maintenance and renewal. The solution lies in the elimination of nuclear weapons and fissile materials. As an interim measure tactical weapons should be eliminated from national arsenals and inventories. Such weapons are meant for nuclear warfighting; and their existence, even under strict control, is incompatible with the international geopolitical situation at the end of the Cold War.

A treaty to prohibit the further production of fissile weapon material will go a long way towards improving control over the future growth of such material and ensure better control over possible diversion. This should be expedited as part of the process to eliminate nuclear weapons. Concurrently, steps need to be taken to reduce drastically the stockpiles of fissile materials in the world. The safety of existing fissile materials could also be improved by introducing a multinational UN security system. This would be an important advance in UN peacekeeping. While interim steps are required to address specific situations, such as the problems emanating from the disintegration of the former Soviet Union, more comprehensive long-term measures also need to be instituted to forestall future illegal trafficking. Serious consideration needs to be given, therefore, to establishing a comprehensive global treaty to ban the smuggling of nuclear materials.

References

1. *Arms Control Today*, November 1993.
2. IAEA Statute, INFCIRC/153, paragraph 2.
3. Broad WJ. *International Herald Tribune*, 22 August 1994.
4. *The Economist*, 26 August 1994.
5. Hibbs M. Plutonium, politics and panic. *Bulletin of the Atomic Scientists* 1994; 50 (6): 24–31.

6. *International Herald Tribune*, 20 December 1994.
7. Kiser JW, Hines J. Monumental nuclear threat. *International Herald Tribune*, 18 August 1994.
8. *International Herald Tribune*, 22 and 26 August 1994.
9. The high price of freeing markets. *The Economist*, 19 February 1994.
10. US Department of Energy, Office of Intelligence and National Security, Office of Threat Assessment. *The Russian Mafia*. 15 November 1993.
11. Bukharin O. Nuclear safeguards and security in the former Soviet Union. *Survival* 1994–95; **36** (4): 57.
12. Izmailov AV. Problems of nuclear facilities and materials physical protection in Russia. Paper presented at INMM Conference, Florida, 1994.
13. Cochran TB. US assistance to improve physical security and accounting of fissile materials in Russia. Paper presented at the Carnegie Endowment for International Peace Conference; Nuclear Non-Proliferation in 1995: Renewal, Transition, or Decline? Washington, 31 January 1995.
14. *The News*, 15 May 1994.

(24 April 1995)

Jasjit Singh has been Director of the New Delhi Institute for Defence Studies and Analyses since 1987. He entered the Indian Air Force in 1954, graduating from its Academy with the Sword of Honour, and held several important commands and received awards before retiring with the rank of Air Commodore. He is one of India's leading strategic experts. He has written and spoken widely on security issues especially relating to Asia, and is a member of the International Commission for Peace and Food, and the Commission for a New Asia.

Correspondence: Institute for Defence Studies and Analyses, Sapru House, Barakhamba Road, New Delhi 110001, India.

Part III

THE FUTURE
WAYS OUT OF THE
NUCLEAR ARMS RACE

Do Nuclear Weapons Have any Rational Utility?

FRANK BARNABY

If the leaders of the nuclear weapon states have their way nuclear weapons will remain of central importance in international affairs for the foreseeable future. The number of tactical and strategic nuclear weapons operationally deployed by the United States and Russia will, according to current plans, be cut from today's total of 50,000 to a total of about 10,000 within the next ten years. Nevertheless, American and Russian political leaders, supported by some of their military leaders, continue to claim that their nuclear weapons have significant utility. And the behaviour of British, French, and Chinese leaders suggests that they also believe that nuclear weapons are useful.

Nuclear Policies of Military and Political Leaders

It is not surprising that some military leaders argue in favour of the continued deployment and modernization of nuclear weapons. After all, some military careers – in, for example, the strategic nuclear submarine fleets – continue to depend on nuclear arsenals. Yet most military officers insist that the decision to use nuclear weapons would generally be a political one, taken for political rather than military reasons.

Because the military now have an arsenal of conventional weapons of various destructive powers, including very powerful ones, which can be delivered with great accuracy, the number of occasions when it could be argued that nuclear weapons are the only (or the best) weapons which can achieve a certain military objective is vanishingly small. The military-technological fact of life is that very powerful conventional weapons can now be delivered with such precision that the use of nuclear weapons can no longer be justified. For this reason some senior military officers are arguing for the abolition of nuclear weapons. Put simply, in today's world nuclear weapons are obsolete. And the moral, legal, military, and political reasons against the use of nuclear weapons are so strong that the use of conventional weapons would be the preferred option under all circumstances.

Even though nuclear weapons have no military utility, the political leaders of the nuclear weapon states continue to rationalize their possession of nuclear weapons by claiming that they improve national – and even global – security. This argument is old hat. Throughout the Cold War,

Western politicians justified their nuclear forces on the grounds that they prevented (i.e., deterred) a major international war – conventional as well as nuclear – in Europe.

And they still argue that nuclear weapons continue to deter conventional and nuclear war in the post-Cold War world. The Warsaw Pact has disappeared but, they say, the world may be even less stable now than it was during the Cold War. The Western nuclear weapon powers argue that they still need nuclear weapons in case Russia again becomes a threat or in case they become involved in a future war in some unstable region in which one of the combatants has nuclear weapons.

Many doubt that nuclear weapons have played any role in preventing war in Europe. But, even if they did, few can really believe that Russia will again become a serious enough threat to require deterring with nuclear weapons. Even those who predict a war between Russia and the Ukraine do not expect it to spread to Europe. Nor is it really credible that the declared nuclear weapon states (the United States, Russia, the United Kingdom, France, and China) will drop nuclear weapons on Third World targets.

There is, of course, a fundamental flaw in the argument used by the nuclear weapon powers. If they claim that nuclear weapons are good for them, they cannot at the same time argue that other countries, like Israel, India, Pakistan, and so on, should not have them too, to increase their security and to deter wars in their regions. It is simply not credible to argue that India, for example, should not have them to deter a nuclear-armed China, the country India sees as its greatest threat. And, of course, if India has nuclear weapons, is not Pakistan justified in wanting a nuclear deterrent too when it is in conflict with a nuclear-capable India over Kashmir?

Now that the American and Russian nuclear arsenals are being reduced, it is being implied that nuclear policies of the great powers are moving to a policy of minimum nuclear deterrence, based on a relatively small nuclear arsenals. But a world containing nations deploying nuclear weapons, albeit a relatively small number of them, cannot be maintained indefinitely. It is most probable that for so long as nuclear weapons remain in national arsenals more countries will acquire them. If large-scale nuclear weapon proliferation is to be avoided, nuclear weapons must be removed from national control, preferably abolished.

To keep nuclear weapons to deter countries which may possibly acquire them in the future is, then, an ineffective policy, likely to encourage the spread of nuclear weapons. The spread of nuclear weapons will reduce the security of all countries, including the declared nuclear weapon powers. Therefore, the concept of a nuclear-weapon-free world is likely to be seen increasingly to be in the national interest of these nuclear weapon powers.

So far as political leaders are concerned, the utility of nuclear weapons may be confined to their mere possession. The use of the weapons may not enter the calculations of political leaders. The political utility of nuclear weapons will not be the same for all the nuclear weapon powers. Take British nuclear weapons as an example. British political leaders may well believe that the political utility of their nuclear weapons are mainly related to Britain's ability to retain its permanent seat on the UN Security Council. This may depend on Britain remaining a nuclear weapon power.

Politicians, among others, are impressed by the fact that all the current permanent members of the Security Council are nuclear weapon states. But they are also aware that Britain's seat is increasingly threatened by Germany and Japan. In the post-Cold War world, economic power reflects international prestige and status more than military nuclear power. As time goes on, nuclear weapons may well count for less and less in the corridors of the United Nations.

Reasons for Acquiring Nuclear Weapons

The most important reasons why countries may acquire nuclear weapons are: prestige; the need to solve real or perceived security threats; and domestic political motives. There is also likely to be a 'domino' effect in some regions.

As described above, prestige may be a central reason why the United Kingdom is keeping and modernizing its nuclear weapons. The same argument probably applies to France. Smaller countries may well see a nuclear weapon force as a way of achieving leadership in their regions. This may explain Iraq's nuclear ambitions.

Political leaders may want to develop nuclear weapons for internal political reasons – to satisfy the demands of the military, to boost domestic political prestige, or to distract the attention of the population from deteriorating social or economic conditions. Some countries have, or perceive that they have, security problems which they believe may be removed, or reduced, by the acquisition of nuclear weapons. India, for example, may have initiated a nuclear weapon programme because of a (perceived?) security threat from a nuclear armed China. And, in turn, Pakistan's nuclear weapon programme may be a reaction to feelings of insecurity produced by India's nuclear capabilities.

Changing Nuclear Policies

History shows that once a country acquires nuclear weapons it will continue to improve them by developing new types and to create increasingly sophisticated delivery systems to carry them. In particular, the accuracy of the delivery of warheads and the reliability of warheads will be steadily improved. These developments will inevitably result in changes in the nuclear policy of the country concerned.

Nuclear policies will change because the targets at which nuclear weapons are aimed depend mainly on the accuracy with which they can be delivered. Inaccurate weapons are seen to be useful to support a policy of nuclear deterrence, by threatening an enemy with unacceptable death and destruction. The targets for such a nuclear deterrence policy are the enemy's cities, civilian population, and industry. These are the hostages to nuclear deterrence.

As the accuracy of delivery of nuclear warheads increases, they become more capable of destroying even very hardened military targets. Adversaries believe that accurate nuclear weapons are targeted on military installations rather than cities; the hostages to deterrence disappear. Nuclear war fighting, based on the destruction of hostile military forces, then becomes the preferred policy. Generally speaking, nuclear policies do not necessarily change because political leaders want to adopt a nuclear-war fighting policy, but because technological developments make change necessary.

Moves away from nuclear deterrence by mutual assured destruction and towards nuclear war fighting explain why many of the nuclear weapon states will not adopt a no-first-use policy, promising not to be the first to use nuclear weapons. In fact, the failure to adopt a no-first-use implies that the country has a nuclear-war fighting policy which may require a pre-emptive first nuclear strike.

(15 May 1995)

The End of the Beginning: Progress towards the Abolition of Nuclear Weapons

VICTOR SIDEL

In 1961 a small group of young Boston physicians met in the living room of Dr Bernard Lown, at that time already a highly respected cardiologist. We came together because of our concern about the threat posed by new bombs of unprecedented power that had been developed and tested by the United States and the Soviet Union during the 1950s. The nuclear bombs that had been dropped on Hiroshima and Nagasaki in 1945, each with an explosive power of approximately fifteen thousand tons of TNT, had been based on nuclear fission: the disintegration of a large atom (uranium-235 or plutonium-239), after absorption of a neutron, into smaller atoms, with the release of enormous energy and the release of a neutron to produce a chain reaction. The bombs tested in the 1950s were based on nuclear fusion: the energy liberated in forming a small nucleus (helium) from the fusion of two even smaller nuclei (isotopes of hydrogen).

The new bombs, called hydrogen bombs or thermonuclear bombs, had an explosive power three physical orders of magnitude – one-thousand-fold – greater than those detonated over Japan. When descriptions of the energy distribution produced by these new weapons and of US government scenarios for use of these to bomb the United States were published in the open literature, the Boston physicians established a small group to analyse the potential health and environmental consequences of the detonation of these weapons. My colleagues and I documented both the short-term and the long-term effects of the unprecedented blast, heat and ionizing radiation that would be produced. The effects included: traumatic injuries from the collapse of buildings, flying debris and the throwing about of humans caused by the blast wave; severe burns and lung damage directly caused by the immediate radiation of heat and by the conflagrations and firestorms the heat wave would ignite; radiation damage caused by the neutron and gamma ray flux from the initial detonation and by alpha, beta and gamma radiation from short-range and long-range fallout of the radionuclides produced; and psychological damage to the survivors. The study group also made estimates of the death or incapacitation of medical personnel and the destruction of medical facilities and medical supplies.

The report of this analysis, published in 1962 in the *New England Journal of Medicine*,[1] concluded that the use of such weapons would be so destructive to human health, to the environment, and to medical personnel and facilities that attempts at response by health workers after the bombs had fallen would be almost entirely futile. The report, which was attributed to a Special Study Section of the group, which had adopted the name Physicians for Social Responsibility (PSR), argued that 'physicians, charged with the responsibility for the lives of their patients and the health of their communities, must also explore a new area of preventive medicine, the prevention of thermonuclear war'.[2]

Shortly after its formation, PSR received an invitation from the Medical Association for the Prevention of War (MAPW) in the United Kingdom, whose formation had antedated that of PSR by a decade, to send a representative to the MAPW Second Conference on the Pathogenesis of War. The conference was held at St Hugh's College, Oxford, in July 1962.[3] It was extremely informative and deeply inspiring, particularly to the PSR representative, the author of this article, and to his spouse. The warm hospitality shown by Dr Duncan Leys (the Chairman of the Conference and of MAPW), Dr Norman MacDonald (who summarized the conference and later led MAPW), Professor LS Penrose, Dr Margaret Penrose, and Dr Alex Poteliakhoff initiated long-lasting personal friendships. That first encounter also established a warm and productive bond between PSR and MAPW (and now MEDACT) that continues to this day.

In 1980 Dr Lown, together with Dr Evgueni Chazov, a leading cardiologist of the Soviet Union, founded the International Physicians for Prevention of Nuclear War. This federation included MAPW and the Medical Campaign Against Nuclear Weapons – now united as Medical Action for Global Security (MEDACT) – in the United Kingdom, the Soviet Physicians for the Prevention of Nuclear War in the then USSR, and PSR in the United States, as well as similar organizations in other countries around the world. The work of IPPNW and its national affiliates was recognized by the Nobel Peace Prize[4] in 1985, with a citation that in part read:

> [IPPNW] has performed a considerable service to mankind by spreading authoritative information and by creating an awareness of the catastrophic consequences of nuclear warfare ... This in turn contributes to an increase in the pressure of public opposition to the proliferation of nuclear weapons and to a redefining of priorities, with greater attention being paid to health and other humanitarian issues. Such an awakening of public opinion ... can give the present arms limitation negotiations new perspectives and a new seriousness.

IPPNW now has affiliates in 80 nations that in total claim over 100,000 supporters. It continues to warn against the consequences of the production, testing, stockpiling and use of nuclear weapons. The world's stockpiles had increased to some 50,000 nuclear weapons, with an explosive power equivalent to fifteen billion tons of TNT, three tons of TNT for every human being on the planet. Although the number of weapons and the explosive force in the stockpiles has decreased somewhat in the past few years, detonation of even a small fraction of these bombs would cause catastrophic environmental damage. The damage would include short-term problems that massive fires and short-lived radionuclides produced by the nuclear detonation would cause in the ecosystem and long-term problems caused by long-lived radionuclides, such as plutonium with a radioactive half-life of 24,000 years. There is also a potential for a 'nuclear winter', a precipitous drop in surface temperatures on a regional or global scale as a result of millions of metric tons of soot injected by mass fires into the upper atmosphere, blocking sunlight and absorbing heat. Even the modest temperature drop predicted by some calculations (which some have called 'nuclear autumn') would be sufficient to cause serious disruption of agriculture, threatening the survivors with malnutrition or famine.[5]

There is also potential damage from widespread ionizing radiation to human immune systems leading to epidemics of uncontrollable infectious disease, and potential damage to the human gene pool with consequences for generations yet unborn. In addition to this damage to human beings and to human gene pools, the incremental international efforts of the past two decades to protect biodiversity and non-human gene pools could be dashed in just a few days.[6] IPPNW has noted that these world-wide environmental and ecological consequences, harming people and the environment in non-belligerent as well as belligerent nations, would be violations of a fundamental principle of international law.

Even if use of nuclear weapons is limited to military targets, such as command bunkers and missile silos, weapons of large yield are likely to be detonated at ground level. Such use would produce even greater radioactive fallout than would be the result of airbursts over cities; the fallout would cause damage to humans hundreds and even thousands of miles from the site of the attack. Such consequences, even if 'collateral' to attacks on military targets, would affect the people of neutral nations and therefore are contrary to international law.

The damage that the use of nuclear weapons would cause to medical personnel and medical facilities is a violation of the Geneva Conventions of 1949 and therefore a clear violation of international law. The 1987 World Health Organization (WHO) report, *Effects of Nuclear War on Health and Health Services*, stated that the use of even a single nuclear weapon would overwhelm any health service, inflict indiscriminate and inhumane suffering on innocent civilians, and cause widespread and long-term environmental destruction that would affect many future generations. The report went on to state that, since no health service in the world could adequately cope with the casualties resulting from the use of even a single nuclear weapon, 'the only possible solution is primary prevention; that is, the prevention of nuclear war'. Since the WHO Constitution states that, 'the attainment of the highest possible level of health is a fundamental human right', surely the indiscriminate destruction of medical personnel and facilities and the massive increase in injury, disease, disability and death caused by the use of nuclear weapons would therefore represent a clear violation of rights specified by the WHO Constitution.

IPPNW has also pointed out that the use of nuclear weapons is likely to cause greatest injury to noncombatant populations and especially those most vulnerable – infants, the elderly and the infirm – a direct violation of yet another fundamental principle of international law.

In sum, IPPNW and its affiliates have argued that the use of nuclear weapons would constitute a public health and environmental disaster. Representatives of IPPNW and of other groups – including the International Association of Lawyers Against Nuclear Arms and the International Peace Bureau – therefore worked with delegates to the World Health Assembly, the governing body of WHO, which had in 1987 declared that 'the role of physicians and other health workers in the preservation and promotion of peace is the most significant factor for the attainment of health for all'.[7] On 14 May 1993 the 46th World Health Assembly adopted resolution WHA46.40 ('Health and Environmental Effects of Nuclear Weapons') that instructed the Director-General of WHO, as a specialized agency of the United Nations, to request an advisory opinion from the International Court of Justice (the 'World Court') in The Hague:

> In view of the health and environmental effects, would the use of nuclear weapons by a State in war or other armed conflict be a breach of its obligations under international law including the WHO constitution?

More recently, the nations affiliated with the Non-Aligned Movement initiated a resolution, adopted by the United Nations General Assembly, asking the court to declare illegal both the use and the threat of use of nuclear weapons. Over 100 million people around the world, including 43 million people in Japan alone, signed declarations of conscience on this question; I personally had the privilege, as Co-President of IPPNW, of participating in the presentation of the signatures to the World Court at the Peace Palace in The Hague.

Work on the World Court Project is only one of the ways in which IPPNW is working for the abolition of nuclear weapons. Abolition has been the ultimate goal of IPPNW since its founding. At the IPPNW International Council meeting in October 1993 a decision was made to initiate immediate activities directed at abolition of nuclear weapons, with the goal of negotiating a convention banning the development, production, testing, stock piling, transfer or use of nuclear weapons by the year 2000.

To this end, IPPNW joined with other non-governmental organizations at the Nuclear Non-Proliferation Treaty Review and Extension Conference in New York City in April–May 1995 to issue a call to all states – particularly the nuclear weapon states, declared and *de facto* – to take the following steps:

1. Initiate in 1995 and conclude by the year 2000 negotiations on a nuclear weapons abolition convention that requires the phased elimination of all nuclear weapons within a timebound framework, with provisions for effective verification and enforcement.
2. Immediately make an unconditional pledge not to use or threaten to use nuclear weapons.
3. Rapidly complete a truly comprehensive test ban treaty with a zero threshold and with the stated purpose of precluding nuclear weapons development by all states.
4. Cease to produce and deploy new and additional nuclear weapon systems, and commence to withdraw and disable deployed nuclear weapon systems.
5. Prohibit the military and commercial production and reprocessing of all weapons-usable radioactive materials.
6. Subject all weapons-usable radioactive materials and nuclear facilities in all states to international accounting, monitoring, and safeguards, and establish a public international registry of all weapons-usable radioactive materials.
7. Prohibit nuclear weapons research, design, development, and testing through laboratory experiments including but not limited to non-nuclear hydrodynamic explosions and computer simulations, subject all nuclear weapons laboratories to international monitoring, and close all nuclear test sites.
8. Create additional nuclear weapons free zones such as those established by the treaties of Tlatelolco and Rarotonga.
9. Recognize and declare the illegality of threat or use of nuclear weapons, publicly and before the World Court.
10. Establish an international energy agency to promote and support the development of sustainable and environmentally safe non-nuclear energy sources.
11. Create mechanisms to ensure the participation of citizens and NGOs in planning and monitoring the process of nuclear weapons abolition.

In sum, IPPNW urges the nations of the world that possess nuclear weapons to destroy their stockpiles as rapidly as possible and to pledge that these weapons will never again be used under any circumstances. IPPNW also urges the nations of the world that do not possess nuclear weapons to refrain from acquiring them and to insist that all nations declare by solemn agreement that nuclear weapons will be abolished by a defined deadline in the near future.

Abolition of nuclear weapons – like the abolition of human slavery over a century ago – is within our grasp. As an example, in July 1994 a top US military officer – Air Force General Charles A. Horner, who as head of the

US North American Aerospace Defense Command is responsible for defending the United States and Canada against nuclear weapons – publicly called for the abolition of nuclear weapons. He said, 'The nuclear weapon is obsolete; I want to get rid of them all.' 'Think of the high moral ground we secure by having none,' he continued. 'It's kind of hard for us to say to North Korea, "You are terrible people, you're developing a nuclear weapon" when the United States has thousands of them.' This is the first time to our knowledge that a high-ranking US military officer on active duty has made such an explicit statement calling for abolition.

In addition to attempts to prevent nuclear war and to abolish nuclear weapons, IPPNW is concerned with the prevention of the use of other weapons of mass destruction and with prevention of war itself. IPPNW helped in the development of the Chemical Weapons Convention which, upon its ratification by a sufficient number of countries, will prohibit the development, production, testing, stockpiling, transfer or use of chemical weapons. IPPNW has a role in attempts to strengthen the Biological Weapons Convention. IPPNW supports the work of the Commission on Disarmament Education, sponsored by the International Association of University Presidents and the United Nations Center for Disarmament Affairs, which attempts to introduce material on disarmament and prevention of war into the curricula of universities throughout the world. The curriculum for medical schools, entitled 'Medicine and Peace', is in part based on curricula developed by PSR and IPPNW.

IPPNW also addresses the root causes of growing insecurity in the world through additional advocacy programmes and partnerships. Specifically, IPPNW works closely with its affiliates in the South as active partners in the campaign for abolition by locating the campaign within the broader paradigm of common security. UNICEF has called the 1980s 'The Decade of Despair'. For the world's poorest people, average incomes have dropped by 10 per cent to 25 per cent. Today more than one billion – one in every five – live in absolute poverty. In the 37 poorest countries, spending on health has been reduced by 50 per cent and on education by 25 per cent. In over 50 nations, primary school enrollment has been falling.

IPPNW has long recognized that 'destruction before detonation', the diversion of enormous human and financial resources to the arms race, is one of the major causes of delayed economic development and of poverty.[8] For this reason, many of us in IPPNW believe, it must give high priority to sustainable development, cancellation of the debts claimed by the nations of the 'North' against the nations of the South, and elimination of world poverty. We must call upon the nations of the world, particularly the rich nations that profit from the poverty of the poor nations, to recognize that the health, well-being and security of the people of the North depends increasingly upon the health, well-being and security of the people of the South and to change their economic, military and political policies so as to close the gap between the haves and the have-nots, between the powerful and the powerless. To emphasize its dedication to these goals IPPNW has added a third co-president from the South to its co-presidents from East and West.

In 1995 IPPNW issued its 'Call for the Abolition of Nuclear Weapons' and solicited signers throughout the world. The Call reads:

> Since the first nuclear weapon exploded fifty years ago, humanity has had to face the threat of mass destruction. Even a single nuclear bomb exploding in an inhabited area – whether through accident, terrorism, or war – could kill hundreds of thousands of civilians. There is no effective medical response to a nuclear explosion; the only effective approach is prevention.

Even if all existing arms control treaties are fully implemented, in the year 2003 approximately 20,000 warheads will remain – the equivalent of 200,000 Hiroshima bombs. The global devastation from their combined blast, burn, radiation, and environmental effects would be so great that all human civilization could be destroyed.

We cannot accept that the danger of these weapons of mass destruction persists. Furthermore, as long as some states possess nuclear weapons, others will inevitably seek to acquire them.

We call on the nations of the world, and especially on the nuclear weapon states, to enter into negotiations to abolish nuclear weapons. We call on them to pledge themselves to complete these negotiations by the year 2000 so that we can enter the new millennium with a treaty in place committing the world to a firm timetable for the permanent elimination of nuclear weapons.

In its Nobel Prize-honoured work IPPNW follows in a great tradition. The physician, humanist and Nobel Peace laureate Albert Schweitzer wrote that 'nuclear weapons are against international law and they have to be abolished', but he also warned that 'all negotiations regarding the abolition of atomic weapons remain without success because no international public opinion exists which demands this abolition'. His friend Albert Einstein, a Nobel laureate in Physics, warned us that 'the explosive force of nuclear fission has changed everything except our modes of thinking and thus we drift toward unparalleled catastrophe. We shall require an entirely new pattern of thinking,' he said, 'if mankind is to survive.' To this warning Dr Bernard Lown, IPPNW founding co-president, who together with Dr Evgueni Chazov accepted the Nobel Prize on behalf of IPPNW, has added, 'The new way of thinking must be an awakening – to our common origins, to our shared problems, as well as to our common fate. If we are to prevail, we must never delegate in the presence of challenge and never whisper in the presence of wrong.'[9]

References

1. Special Study Section, Physicians for Social Responsibility. The medical consequences of thermonuclear war. *New England Journal of Medicine* 1962; **266**: 1126–1155.
2. Sidel VW, Geiger HJ, Lown B. The medical consequences of thermonuclear war. II. The physicians's role in the post-attack period. *New England Journal of Medicine* 1962; **266**: 1137–1145.
3. The pathogenesis of war. *Lancet* 1962; ii:193–194.
4. Lown B. Nobel Peace Prize lecture: A prescription for hope. *New England Journal of Medicine* 1986; **314**: 985–987.
5. Turco RP, Toon OB, Ackerman TP, Pollack JB, Sagan C. Climate and smoke: an appraisal of nuclear winter. *Science* 1990; **247**: 166–176.
6. Ehrlich PR *et al.* Long-term biological consequences of nuclear war. *Science* 1983; **222**: 1293–1300.
7. World Health Assembly Resolution WHA 34.38, 1987. Cited in Sidel VW. Weapons of mass destruction: The greatest threat to public health. *Journal of the American Medical Association* 1989; **262**: 680–682.
8. Sidel VW. Destruction before detonation. *Lancet* 1985; ii: 1287–1289.
9. Lown B. *Never Whisper in the Presence of Wrong: Selection from Speeches on Nuclear War and Global Survival.* Cambridge, Mass: International Physicians for the Prevention of Nuclear War, 1993.

(11 May 1995)

Victor Sidel is Distinguished University Professor of Social Medicine at Albert Einstein College of Medicine. He was a founding member of Physicians for Social Responsibility and has been its president; he is now co-president of International Physicians for Prevention of Nuclear War and heads its delegation as a non-governmental organization at the United Nations New York City site.

Correspondence: Montefiore Medical Center, 111 East 210 Street, Bronx, New York 10467–2490, USA.

Nuclear Weapons: The Legality Issue

ROB GREEN

Soon after becoming United Kingdom Chair of the World Court Project*
(WCP) in October 1991, I found fascinating parallels between it and the
British campaign to abolish slavery. By chance I discovered the direct
descendant of Thomas Clarkson living two miles from me. William
Wilberforce is generally credited with having led the antislavery movement. However I quickly learned that, while Wilberforce was the parlia-
mentary champion, Clarkson conceived the campaign and drove it
through. In so doing British public opinion was mobilized for the first time
on a human rights issue. And despite taking forty-eight years (1785–1833),
the campaign succeeded.[1]

What surprised me was that he homed in on the *illegality* of slavery. It
all began at St John's College, Cambridge, when he wrote a prize-winning
essay on the question: 'Is it lawful to make slaves of others against
their will?' In a notoriously cruel world where life was cheap, it was the
illegality which finally forced politicians to vote against a system which
underpinned the nation's economy. (Incidentally, Wilberforce was MP for
Hull – the only major British port not dependent upon the slave trade.
Politicians do not change ...)

On horseback, without telephone, fax or photocopier, Clarkson toured
the country setting up committees in every major city. A million signatures
were collected on petitions from a population of less than 20 million, most
of them illiterate. Meanwhile the slavers used all the pro-nuclear lobby's
arguments: 'a necessary evil', 'cost-effective', 'no alternative', and 'not
against the law'.

The WCP is out to emulate the anti-slavery campaign – and the British
people seem to like the analogy. Instead of petitions, however, individually
signed Declarations of Public Conscience are being collected world-wide
and sent to the International Court of Justice, or World Court. These are
new, and invoke the 'de Martens' clause from the 1907 Hague
Convention,[2] drafted by one of the first Russian writers on international
law, Frederic de Martens (1845–1909). The following clause appears in
the preamble:

> Until a more complete code of the laws of war has been issued, the
> high contracting parties deem it expedient to declare that, in cases
> not included in the Regulations adopted by them, the inhabitants and
> the belligerents remain under the protection and the rule of the

* The World Court Project is an international citizens' initiative to seek advisory opinions
  from the International Court of Justice confirming that the threat or use of nuclear
  weapons is illegal.

principles of the law of nations, as they result from the usages established among civilized peoples, from the laws of humanity, and the
dictates of the public conscience (emphasis added).

What this means is that the 'dictates of the public conscience' must be
taken into account when judging the legal status of a new weapon. Only
World Court judges can do that; but ordinary citizens can say whether
they think a weapon is *right or wrong* – and these decisions should be
linked.

Harnessing public conscience and the law is proving potent again in
reining in the same three former great slaving nations – the United States,
United Kingdom and France. On 15 December 1994 the WCP had its
biggest breakthrough yet. It persuaded the United Nations (UN) General
Assembly to ask the World Court for an urgent advisory opinion on the
question: 'Is the threat or use of nuclear weapons in any circumstance permitted under international law?'

Despite desperate countermoves by the three North Atlantic Treaty
Organization's nuclear weapon states (Russia quietly voted with them,
while China did not vote), this historic resolution was passed by 78 votes
to 43, with 38 abstentions and 26 not voting. The high number of states
keeping their heads down shows how controversial it was. For the first
time since the creation of the UN almost fifty years ago, the legality of the
unwritten qualification for permanent membership of the Security Council
had been challenged.

The nuclear cartel have more than that to fear. Their nuclear deterrence
policies will now stand trial in the highest court in the world – and the
prosecution case is damning. A World Court opinion outlawing nuclear
weapon threat or use would not be enforceable. However, nuclear
weapons would be given the same stigma as chemical and biological
weapons. The Royal Navy would have to review the legality of Polaris and
Trident patrols. International pressure would mount for rapid progress to
a Nuclear Weapons Convention, using the widely-acclaimed Chemical
Weapons Convention as a blueprint.

As with the abolition of slavery, behind this lies a story epitomizing
Margaret Mead's words: 'Never doubt that a small group of thoughtful,
committed citizens can change the world. Indeed, it's the only thing that
ever has.'

The Gestation of the WCP

The question of banning nuclear weapons was implicit in the UN's first
resolution, Resolution 1(1) unanimously adopted by the UN General
Assembly on 24 January 1946 to establish an international atomic energy
commission. This included a clause 'for the elimination from national
armaments of atomic weapons and of all other major weapons of mass

destruction'. The Cold War froze out further attempts to act on it. Nevertheless, since 1961 the overwhelming majority of states have regularly voted in the General Assembly that the use of nuclear weapons would be a crime against humanity. For example, in 1992 Resolution 47/53c was adopted by 125 votes to 21, with 22 abstentions and 16 not voting.

In 1969 Sean MacBride, a former Irish foreign affairs minister, senior UN civil servant and human rights lawyer and winner of the 1974 Nobel Peace Prize while President of the International Peace Bureau (IPB), wrote:

> The [1925] Geneva [Gas] Protocol was drawn up before the discovery of atomic power, and today the damage which indiscriminate use of such energy could cause is out of all proportion to military requirements. There is of course the view that no use of nuclear weapons can be justified, and that the total prohibition of such weapons in warfare should form a separate convention or part of a non-proliferation treaty.[3]

He brought his thinking on the problem to fruition in the London Nuclear Warfare Tribunal, which he organized and chaired in 1985, but sadly died before its report was published.[4] The tribunal, which included US international law expert Professor Richard Falk, concluded that 'current and planned [nuclear] weapons developments, strategies and deployments violate the basic rules and principles of international law'.

In 1987 MacBride launched a Lawyers Appeal which called for the prohibition of nuclear weapons. It declared that the use of a nuclear weapon would constitute a violation of international law and human rights, and a crime against humanity. By 1992 this appeal had been signed by 11,000 lawyers from 56 countries, including two of the judges at the World Court.

Meanwhile, in 1986 Richard Falk was invited to Aotearoa/New Zealand† by its Foundation for Peace Studies to speak on nuclearism and international law. Two years earlier, a Labour government led by David Lange had been elected with a mandate to outlaw nuclear weapons and power in Aotearoa. Harold Evans, a retired Christchurch magistrate, picked up Falk's idea of a WCP-type approach, and never looked back.

Labour Pains

With supporting testimony from Falk and five other distinguished international lawyers, Evans wrote an open letter to the Aotearoa/NZ and Australian Prime Ministers in March 1987, three months before the New Zealand nuclear-free bill became law.[5] In it he challenged them to sponsor a UN resolution to seek a World Court opinion on 'the legality or otherwise of nuclear weaponry'. He followed it up with appeals to all 71 UN member states with diplomatic representation in Canberra and Wellington.

Australian Prime Minister Robert Hawke rejected the idea, but Lange

† The names Aotearoa and New Zealand are used interchangeably. The former is the original name, the latter the European name. Both are official.

showed real interest. A long dialogue ensued, strongly backed by the newly-formed Public Advisory Committee on Disarmament and Arms Control (PACDAC). Among other things, this unique body was required by the Nuclear Free Act to monitor implementation of the act. However, it lacked the clout to prevail over reactionary foreign affairs officials on this issue.

Undeterred, Evans set about mobilizing citizen support, especially among anti-nuclear lawyers and doctors. Dr Robin Briant was a PACDAC member. As NZ Chair of International Physicians for the Prevention of Nuclear War (IPPNW), she arranged for him to address them in March 1989, and later that year they passed an Aotearoa/NZ-sponsored resolution through IPPNW's World Congress.

Meanwhile a PACDAC Peace Foundation representative, Katie Boanas-Dewes, was chosen by the government to be one of two non-governmental organization members of the NZ delegation to the May 1988 UN Special Session on Disarmament in New York. She had worked on peace issues with Evans since 1979, and organized Richard Falk's Christchurch visit.

In his UN speech, NZ Foreign Minister Russell Marshall made a non-committal reference to the idea; but Boanas-Dewes took her chance when addressing the UN on behalf of Aotearoa/NZ NGOs, saying:

> We strongly urge all nations and peace groups to support a move by jurists in New Zealand and other countries to have the International Court of Justice give an advisory opinion on whether or not nuclear arms are illegal. The symbolic power of such a ruling would be immense ...

Evans now took his cause to Europe. At its annual conference in Brighton in September 1989, the International Peace Bureau endorsed his strategy. The newly-formed International Association of Lawyers Against Nuclear Arms (IALANA) followed suit a few weeks later at its first World Congress in The Hague. Meanwhile, Sweden's Disarmament Ambassador, Maj-Britt Theorin discussed possible co-sponsorship of a UN resolution with her NZ opposite number Fan Wilde, but Labour lost the 1990 NZ election.

WCP is Born

In March 1991 another Aotearoa citizen arrived in New York, representing NGOs worldwide opposing the Gulf War. Alyn Ware, then a 29-year-old ex-kindergarten teacher and peace activist, approached several UN missions with the WCP idea, and found support. Three months later Boanas-Dewes and IPB Secretary-General Colin Archer had a similar response from eight missions in Geneva. Boanas-Dewes then visited the UK, where she helped mobilize a strong group led by Keith Mothersson which was already working on the idea sown by Evans in 1989. It was

Mothersson who organized an obscure meeting in London on 12 October 1991 which I attended as an observer for Just Defence – from which I emerged as the dazed first Chair of WCP(UK)! Plunging into a crash course on international law and the World Court, I soon realized it could be a winner.

The doctors, lawyers and peace activists came together in Geneva for the WCP's international launch in May 1992. An International Steering Committee was formed of representatives of the three principal co-sponsoring NGOs (IPPNW, IALANA and IPB) with Boanas-Dewes and myself. Alyn Ware returned to New York as a volunteer with the Lawyers' Committee on Nuclear Policy (LCNP, the US affiliate of IALANA), and later became its Director.

World Health Organization Breakthrough

Just before the May 1992 launch, Dr Erich Geiringer and IPPNW(NZ) masterminded an attempt to table a WCP resolution in the annual assembly of the World Health Organization (WHO). Exploiting IPPNW's excellent contacts in the WHO bureaucracy and member states' health ministries, the move failed mainly because the resolution was not formally on the agenda. Learning from this, support for the resolution was gained in time for it to be tabled properly the next year. On 14 May 1993 the resolution was passed by a big majority despite heavy pressure from the NATO nuclear cartel. It asked the World Court:

> In view of the health and environmental effects, would the use of nuclear weapons by a state in war or other armed conflict be a breach of its obligations under international law including the WHO Constitution?

After some delay, the question was received by the Court in September 1993.

The World Court and Advisory Opinions

The International Court of Justice, which sits in the Peace Palace at The Hague, is the principal judicial organ of the UN and the supreme tribunal ruling on questions of international law. Its jurisdiction is governed by its Statute, which is an integral part of the UN Charter.[6]

The Court comprises 15 judges drawn from the different legal systems of the world. The UN General Assembly and Security Council simultaneously and independently elect them for nine years

> regardless of their nationality from persons of high moral character, who possess the qualifications required in their respective countries

for appointment to the highest judicial offices, or are juriconsults of recognized competence in international law.[7]

They are under oath to act impartially and conscientiously. They are paid by the General Assembly. As a general practice, however, there are nearly always judges from the permanent members of the Security Council.

The Court's two functions are to decide legal disputes between states (known as contentious cases), and to give advisory opinions. The General Assembly may request an advisory opinion on any legal question. Other UN organs and specialized agencies (such as the WHO) may also request opinions on legal questions arising within the scope of their activities.[8] While advisory opinions themselves are not binding on governments, an advisory opinion on the questions put by the WHO and UN General Assembly would provide a definitive clarification of the law on this issue, and would carry unrivalled authority.

Nuclear Weapons and the Law

International treaties and agreements such as the Hague Conventions, Geneva Conventions, Genocide Convention and Nuremberg Principles prohibit the use of weapons which:

- cause unnecessary suffering to combatants and indiscriminate harm to civilians
- release poison or analogous liquids, materials or devices
- affect neutral states
- cause widespread, severe and long-term environmental damage, or
- are disproportionately destructive compared to the military objective.

Nuclear weapons do all these. Furthermore, chemical and biological weapons, though far less destructive than nuclear weapons, are already prohibited by specific international conventions. However, UN General Assembly resolutions do not have binding force. Hence nuclear weapons states, in justifying their nuclear arsenals, claim that there is no international law which specifically bans nuclear weapons.

Nevertheless, the nuclear weapon states are all parties to the Hague and Geneva Conventions and, apart from China, have affirmed the Nuremberg Principles. They are therefore bound to abide by these conventions and norms. Four of the nuclear weapon states (the United States, Union of Soviet Socialist Republics, France and the United Kingdom) were the principal creators of the Nuremberg Principles in 1946 (China did not vote for the affirmation of the principles in UN Resolution 1 (95) of 1946 because the People's Republic of China did not then occupy the seat). Thus, if the Court decides that the threat or use of nuclear weapons violates these conventions and principles, all parties to them will be bound to recognize this.

Furthermore Article VI.2 of the US Constitution, for example, provides that international law shall be part of 'the supreme law of the land'. In the United Kingdom 'the (customary) law of nations in its fullest extent is and forms part of the law of England'.[9]

Citizens' Evidence at the Court

The Court normally allows only governments or UN agencies to present evidence. However, in the Peace Palace on 10 June 1994 I was in a citizens' delegation welcomed by the Court Registrar. Representing over 700 NGOs which have endorsed the WCP, we presented a unique collection of documents, including:

- 170,000 Declarations of Public Conscience
- a sample of the 100 million signatures to the Appeal from Hiroshima and Nagasaki
- the 11,000 signature MacBride Lawyers' Appeal Against Nuclear Weapons
- material surveying 50 years of citizens' opposition to nuclear weapons.

In accepting these into the Court archive, the Registrar undertook to draw the judges' attention to them when considering the case. He took care to point out that they had not been accepted as legal evidence. Nonetheless, it is believed that this is the first time that the Court has accepted material from a citizens' delegation. It indicates that the Court acknowledges the strength of public concern worldwide about the issue.

WCP 22, Nuclear Cartel 9

Taking up the saga from September 1993, the Court allowed states until 20 September 1994 to make submissions on the WHO question. It announced that 35 submissions had been received.[10] This was an unusually large total, and some 26 more than the nuclear cartel wanted. Judge Mohammed Bedjaoui, President of the Court, in an address to the UN General Assembly on 13 October 1994, said:

> [The WHO] request, raising as it does some serious issues, has prompted much concern in the international community judging by the unusual number of States ... which have submitted written statements to us.

The indications are that only five non-nuclear states (Australia, Finland, Germany, Italy and the Netherlands) made submissions echoing the line taken by the NATO nuclear trio and Russia (China opted out). Of the remainder, 22 argued that any nuclear weapon use would be illegal, one (Ireland) wanted the question answered, and three (Aotearoa/NZ, Japan and Norway) were on the fence. Submitting states received a copy of every other submission, and were given until 20 June 1995 to comment in writing on them. Eight states did so: the United States, Russia, the United Kingdom and France were balanced by India, Malaysia, Nauru and the Solomon Islands.

WCP Challenges Nuclear Deterrence

A major objection by the NATO nuclear states, and the Australian and Aotearoa/NZ governments, was that the UN General Assembly, not the WHO, was the correct forum for the WCP issue. Accordingly Alyn Ware, working with LCNP Co-Presidents Peter Weiss and Saul Mendlovitz, approached several UN missions in New York following the WHO success. Led by Zimbabwe's Foreign Minister, the Non-Aligned Movement (NAM) – 111 of the UN's 185 member states – agreed to table a more ambitious resolution at the 1993 General Assembly disarmament session.

The last week of October 1993 saw a struggle in the General Assembly's First Committee. Zimbabwe, backed by a determined group of South Pacific states, lobbied hard, helped by a WCP team which included Alyn Ware, Katie Boanas-Dewes, Maori elder Pauline Tangiora, Australian QC Edward St John and myself. After some crucial lobbying by Vanuatu's Ambassador Robert Van Lierop, supported by ex-Health Minister Hilda Lini, the resolution was introduced reluctantly by the NAM Chair, Indonesia.

The United States, United Kingdom and France sent delegations to many NAM capitals threatening trade and aid if the resolution was not withdrawn. On 19 November the NAM consensus buckled, and Indonesia announced that action on it had been deferred. However, every UN member government now knew about the WCP, and how it threatened the privileged position of the nuclear weapon states.[11]

The WCP International Steering Committee, meeting in Geneva in May 1994, held out little hope that the NAM would risk further loss of face by trying again that autumn. Three weeks later a momentous fax arrived. NAM Foreign Ministers meeting in Cairo had decided not just to re-table the resolution, but to put it to a vote! The spotlight then swung across to The Hague and the WHO case until late September. Ware gave hints from New York of a struggle within NAM not to falter. Only Benin decided to oppose it; and the NAM forged on to what must surely be their finest moment so far.

The British government tried to stem the anti-nuclear tide, but showed no sign of having thought through the implications. It had the gall to claim that the resolution risked 'being seen as a deliberate attempt to exert pressure over the Court to prejudice its response [to the WHO question] ... [it] can do nothing to further global peace and security'. The French showed signs of hysteria: 'It is a blatant violation of the UN Charter. It goes against the law. It goes against reason' – from the government responsible for the *Rainbow Warrior* atrocity.

Next Steps at the Court

Because the General Assembly question is urgent, the Court received it from the UN Secretary-General within two working days. On 27 June 1995 it announced that 27 states had made submissions on the General Assembly question.[12] The smaller total reflects its greater sensitivity: however, 7 new states made submissions, all of them assessed to be supportive of the WCP (Bosnia, Burundi, Ecuador, Egypt, Lesotho, Qatar and San Marino). Aotearoa/NZ announced that this time it had made a substantive submission, probably arguing for illegality. With Australia failing to make a submission, the WCP effectively held the line by a probable majority of 18 to 8 plus one (Japan) still on the fence. The Court will consider the WHO and General Assembly questions separately but simultaneously. Public hearings will start on 30 October 1995 for 2–6 weeks; and an advisory opinion could be given by the end of the year.

The judges will come under severe pressure from the NATO nuclear states to drop the case because it is 'hypothetical and political' and challenges their security policy. Almost any opinion would cause them grave problems.

There have been dire warnings from some cynical commentators. For example, the Wellington *Evening Post* has reported that the US Ambassador to New Zealand, Josiah Beeman, asked: 'What would happen if the Court ruled they were legal? ... Would New Zealand be prepared to be in violation of a decision of the ICJ by keeping tactical nuclear weapons out of your country when the World Court has declared they are legal?'[13]

Nevertheless, it is certain that the Court will *not* decide that any threat or use of nuclear weapons would be legal. Under existing treaties and conventions, even a gun can be used only in accordance with the laws of war by one combatant against another. And, as already mentioned, in the case of chemical weapons any use of these weapons of mass destruction is illegal. For biological weapons, any use is condemned in the preamble of the Biological Weapons Convention.

While the definition of threat is open to wide interpretation, at the very least the judges will outlaw any use of all but very low-yield nuclear weapons in tightly constrained scenarios. This will discredit the rationale for deterrence, challenge the legality of (for example) ballistic missile submarine patrols, and highlight the military uselessness of nuclear weapons.

Keeping the Judges Straight

Michael Mansfield QC is a British legal champion of the WCP. He gained fame as the lawyer who had the convictions overturned of the

'Birmingham Six' and other Irish people wrongly accused of bombing atrocities. He is convinced that what kept the judges straight was that they knew the public were watching and knowledgeable, and the media were reporting the proceedings. What the WCP has to do is to convince the World Court judges that the world will be watching them, and that media supportive of the WCP cause will report proceedings and understand the arguments. Much will depend on how well the WCP mobilizes public opinion before October. The French threat to resume testing, together with the focus on the 50th anniversary of the founding of the UN, and the atomic bombings of Hiroshima and Nagasaki, will provide a powerful boost.

Ordinary citizens from around the world have persuaded the UN to rumble nuclear deterrence. Now they have to persuade the United States, British and French governments that outlawing nuclear weapons is the golden bridge to a new system of mutual security based on a just, sustainable world order. There will never be a better opportunity.

References

1. Wilson EG. *Thomas Clarkson: A Biography*. London: Macmillan, 1989.
2. *Respecting the Laws and Customs of War on Land*. Hague Convention IV, 1907.
3. MacBride S. *The Humanitarian Laws of Armed Conflict*. Memorandum submitted to the International Conference on Chemical and Biological Warfare, London, 21–23 November 1969.
4. Swedish Lawyers Against Nuclear Arms. *The Bomb and the Law*. Stockholm: Alva and Gunnar Myrdal Foundation, 1989.
5. *The New Zealand Nuclear Free Zone, Disarmament, and Arms Control Act*. Wellington: Government of New Zealand, 1987.
6. Article 92. *Charter of the United Nations*. New York: UN Department of Public Information, 1945.
7. Article 2. *Statute of the International Court of Justice*. New York: UN Department of Public Information, 1945.
8. Article 96. *Charter of the United Nations*. New York: UN Department of Public Information, 1945.
9. *Barbuit's Case*. 1735 25 ER 777.
10. *Communique No 95/17*. The Hague: International Court of Justice, 27 June 1995.
11. Green R. World Court Project: Nuclear Drug Cartel at Bay. *Med War* 1994; 10: 149–52.
12. *Communique No 95/18*. The Hague: International Court of Justice, 27 June 1995.
13. *Evening Post*, Wellington, 15 December 1994.

(15 April 1995)

Commander Rob Green RN (Ret'd) is UK Chair of the World Court Project.
Correspondence: 2 Chiswick House, High Street, Twyford, Berks RG10 9AG.

Part IV

THE GOAL
A NUCLEAR-WEAPON-FREE WORLD

A Nuclear-Weapon-Free World:
The Essential Lesson of Hiroshima

JOSEPH ROTBLAT

Was Hiroshima Necessary?

Fifty years after Hiroshima – and the question whether the use of the atom bomb was justified is still being debated. The official view is that it saved many American lives by bringing the war to a quick end. But according to other views a Japanese offer to surrender was rejected because the United States was determined to demonstrate to the Soviets its newly acquired overwhelming military power.

Hiroshima and Nagasaki are the only two instances when nuclear weapons were used in combat, although their production and testing have taken a terrible toll in human lives, pollution of the environment, and ruinous expenditure. More than 2,000 bombs have been exploded in tests, carried out in the atmosphere, underwater or underground. The explosive power of the atmospheric tests is equivalent to 30,000 Hiroshima bombs, and several million people, in all parts of the world, mainly in future generations, will die from illnesses related to the radioactive fallout from the tests.

Universal Desire for a Nuclear-Weapon-Free World

The iniquitous characteristics of nuclear weapons – enormous destructive power, indiscriminate killing of civilian populations, a legacy of death and disease in people yet unborn – make the atomic bomb repugnant to every rational person. From the beginning there has been a universal desire to eliminate it. The very first resolution of the United Nations, adopted unanimously by the General Assembly in 1946, called for the elimination of nuclear weapons. This call has been repeated time and time again in subsequent declarations and resolutions by the United Nations.

The five nuclear-weapon states became legally committed to nuclear disarmament when they signed the Non-Proliferation Treaty (NPT). Under Article VI of the Treaty they undertook to proceed in good faith to complete nuclear disarmament. This is still their declared objective. Thus, in the UK, the 1994 Statement on the Defence Estimates says: 'Complete and general nuclear disarmament remains a desirable ultimate goal.'[1] But such declarations sound hollow in the light of the actual policies of the nuclear states.

Apart from the general abhorrence of nuclear weapons, their military value, as an instrument of war, has long been disparaged. At their first summit, ten years ago, Ronald Reagan and Mikhail Gorbachev proclaimed the famous dictum: 'A nuclear war cannot be won and must never be fought.' When they met in Reykjavik the following year, they nearly agreed to eliminate nuclear weapons.

The Nuclear Arms Race

The above goes to show that a nuclear-weapon-free world (NWFW) is not a weird idea of a fringe group, but the desired objective of the world community as well as of some world leaders. All the same it could not be considered seriously during the Cold War period. The world was polarized. The two superpowers were locked in a mortal, ideological struggle, in which nuclear weapons played a major role. The whole period was dominated by the relentless nuclear arms race.

One hears nowadays voices hankering for the 'stability' of the Cold War period, as compared with the current state of chaos and uncertainty. But there never was any stability in the military sense. At no time was either side satisfied that its nuclear arsenal was sufficient to ensure its security and prevent destruction by the enemy. Both sides felt compelled to continue improving their offensive capabilities or develop new defensive capabilities. As time went on, the race became extremely costly, imposing unbearable economic burdens, particularly on the Soviet Union. In this author's opinion, had the nuclear arms race continued it would have ended in a nuclear holocaust, with the destruction of our civilization. Fortunately a sane leader emerged: Mikhail Gorbachev, in a very bold move – which later contributed to his downfall – stopped the nuclear arms race.

Are the Nuclear Powers Fulfilling their NPT Obligations?

The collapse of Communism and the disintegration of the Soviet Union created an entirely new political climate: the erstwhile enemies became friends and partners. The main obstacle to a nuclear-weapon-free world has been removed. There was no more excuse for the nuclear powers not to fulfil their obligations under Article VI of the Non-Proliferation Treaty. Yet, they have not embarked on a programme of complete nuclear disarmament. Nuclear deterrence is still considered an essential requisite for security. The recent *Nuclear Posture Review* in the United States concluded: '[the] post-Cold War environment requires the nuclear deterrent',[2] and this is echoed in the policies of Russia, France and the United Kingdom.

In the debate on the extension of the NPT these states kept claiming that they have fulfilled their obligations, pointing to the huge reductions in the arsenals of the United States and Russia under the terms of STARTs I and

II. There is no denying the importance of this action. When, by the year 2003, the START agreements have been implemented, the nuclear arsenals will have been reduced very considerably, and this can only be applauded. But it has little to do with the fulfilment of the obligations under the NPT. The United States and Russia would have made these moves with or without the NPT, because it is in their own interests.

The end of the ideological struggle has enabled the leaders of the super-powers to make a more sensible appraisal of the situation. They have realized that the maintenance of huge nuclear arsenals is expensive and dangerous, and so they have agreed to reduce them, but only to a level which they consider to be necessary for their security. There is no evidence that they intend to proceed to complete nuclear disarmament. Even after START II, about 15,000 nuclear warheads (strategic, tactical and reserve) will still remain. In absolute terms this represents an enormous destructive potential.

As the quotation from the *Nuclear Posture Review*[2] has shown, there has been no change in the basic nuclear policy: nuclear weapons are needed not only to deter a nuclear attack but to deal with other military situations. The United States, United Kingdom and France still reject a No-First-Use policy; and Russia, which pursued this policy under the Soviet regime, has revoked it, thereby confirming that nuclear weapons are needed for purposes other than deterring a nuclear attack.

Summing up, the claim by the nuclear powers that they are fulfilling their NPT commitments is contradicted by their actual policies, which are based on the assumption that nuclear weapons are needed for security. As long as this policy is maintained the nuclear powers will never, or at least not in the foreseeable future, proceed to genuine nuclear disarmament.

The Prestige Factor of Nuclear Weapons Possession

It is important to analyse the reasons given by the nuclear states for the retention of the nuclear deterrent. But, first, one reason should be mentioned which, though important, is not stated openly, indeed it is even denied by them. This is the prestige factor, the high status that the posses-sion of nuclear weapons appears to bestow, a place at the high table. For the United Kingdom and France this was undoubtedly a main reason for starting the development of their atom bombs after the end of the war, but even now it is a strong motivation for keeping them. The argument has also become important for Russia in recent years. After its loss of inter-national standing by the exposure of its economic bankruptcy, Russia clings to nuclear weapons as the last vestige of its past eminence as a superpower. The problem is that other nations, currently non-nuclear, may have the same perception. It is reinforced by the fact – which some say is purely accidental – that the five nuclear-weapon states are the only permanent members of the Security Council with the right of veto. As long as the perception persists that the possession of nuclear weapons gives security and status, this will be a strong motivation for other nations to join the club. It is a recipe for proliferation, and – in a sort of vicious circle – it provides additional motivation for the current nuclear states to retain their arsenals.

Do Nuclear Weapons Prevent War?

One of the stated objections to nuclear disarmament is that nuclear weapons provide stability, they maintain world peace; specifically, that they prevent war. The impression has been created that many potential wars have been avoided by the existence of nuclear weapons. We are led to believe that many wars are waiting to happen, and will happen, as soon as the nuclear arsenals are dismantled; in other words, that a nuclear-weapon-free world would be a very dangerous world.

The argument is largely a remnant of the Cold War propaganda in the West that a war between the East and West would have occurred were it not for the nuclear arsenals of the West. Largely fomented by the powerful lobbies with vested interests in keeping the arms race going, the belief was hatched that the Soviet Union was bent on conquering the world and was waiting for any sign of weakness in the West to pounce. Typical of these notions was the statement made in the House of Commons by William Waldegrave, then a Minister in the Foreign Office: 'Nuclear deterrence has certainly prevented World War – that world war that would otherwise have inevitably broken out sometime, somewhere, after 1945 between America and her allies and Russia and hers.'[3]

One would expect that such a categoric statement would be based on factual evidence, but no such evidence has ever been provided. It has not been provided because it does not exist. Classified Soviet policy documentation, released in recent years, does not contain any evidence that the Soviet Union ever planned to invade the West.[4] It was all a deliberately created myth.

On the other hand, evidence that has become available recently shows that, on at least one occasion, we did come very close to a Third World War, but the danger arose _because_ of the existence of nuclear weapons. The event was the 1962 Cuban Missile Crisis, when the Soviet Union brought nuclear weapons, both strategic and tactical, into Cuba. It is only recently that we have learned[5] how near we were to a nuclear holocaust with the possible destruction of civilization. Thus, far from preventing a world war, nuclear weapons have nearly caused one.

Nevertheless, by constant repetition, assertions of the type made by Mr Waldegrave have become accepted as articles of faith; they have been extrapolated to wars in general, and extended to the post-Cold War period, despite the completely different political climate. Thus, the then Secretary of State for Defence, Malcolm Rifkind, said: 'The value of nuclear weapons ... lies ... not just in deterring the use of weapons by an adversary, but in actually preventing war.'[6] If this were true then nuclear weapons would have to be retained until the likelihood of any war has been eliminated; this means for a very, very long time.

However, there is no more reason to accept Mr Rifkind's statement than that of Mr Waldegrave. The statement is clearly untrue as far as the past is concerned. Wars, many of them bloody, with millions of deaths, have been fought throughout the Cold War period, and have occurred since. Moreover, the nuclear powers themselves were active belligerents in the most bloody of these conflicts: Korea, Vietnam, Cambodia, Afghanistan, Falklands, and the Gulf. And some of these ended with the defeat of the nuclear powers. The possession of nuclear weapons does not appear to have helped them prevent these wars, nor to have given them extra military advantage.

The Risk of Keeping Nuclear Arsenals

On the other hand, the very existence of nuclear weapons is a source of danger: they may be used accidentally, or their use may be threatened by terrorists. There is even the danger of them leading to a nuclear war. Imagine a conventional war between a nuclear and non-nuclear state, like the ones just mentioned. Should the war go badly for the nuclear state, enormous pressure would build up to end the war quickly by dropping a few bombs. When the coffins begin to arrive home, the clamour from the tabloids, who claim to represent the man in the street, may become too strong for a government to resist. But, once used in combat, it could easily escalate into an all-out nuclear war. As Robert McNamara pointed out recently: 'The indefinite combination of human fallibility and nuclear weapons carries a high risk of a potential catastrophe.'[5] This risk will exist as long as nuclear weapons exist, and will increase if more states acquire nuclear weapons. As pointed out, this is likely to happen if the present nuclear states insist on keeping them for their own security.

The Genie is Out of the Bottle

Another argument advanced by the nuclear states as an excuse for retaining their weapons is the 'break-out' syndrome, popularly expressed as 'The genie is out of the bottle.' The United Kingdom's attitude was stated by Malcolm Rifkind: '... nuclear weapons cannot be disinvented. The knowledge exists and cannot be expunged.'[6] If so – the argument goes on – even if agreement has been reached to eliminate all nuclear weapons, this will not prevent a rogue state from building up a new nuclear arsenal some time in the future. In a NWFW this would enable the rogue state to blackmail other countries, perhaps the whole world.

The argument implies that the only remedy against break-out is to retain nuclear arsenals. If this were accepted then the whole objective of the NPT, to achieve nuclear disarmament, would be undermined. We would have to say goodbye to a NWFW. Moreover, the disinvention argument applies not only to nuclear, but also to chemical, biological, even to conventional weapons. It would mean that there should be no disarmament of any kind of weapon.

The fallacy of the disinvention argument is that it ignores other ways by which a civilized society deals with undesirable products of technological advance, by the application of the law; in this case by making the acquisition of nuclear weapons a crime, an illegal act punishable under international law. The nuclear states assume, without providing supporting evidence, that a treaty to eliminate nuclear weapons would not be effective in preventing break-out.

The prevention of break-out is a serious problem. There are many political and military leaders who want to eliminate nuclear weapons, and have not been taken in by the phoney arguments that nuclear weapons help to prevent wars, but are worried about the break-out issue. General Charles Horner, Chief of US Space Command, said: 'The nuclear weapon is obsolete. I want to get rid of them all.'[7] Melvin Laird, a former Secretary of Defense, said: 'A worldwide zero nuclear option with adequate verification should now be our goal ... These weapons ... are useless for military purposes.'[8] And another former Secretary of Defense, Robert McNamara, said: 'I strongly advocate a return, by all nuclear powers, insofar as practicable, to a non-nuclear world,'[5] and he explains that the qualification – insofar as practicable – refers to the necessity of maintaining protection against break-out.

A Nuclear-Weapon-Free World is Feasible

A study of this problem was carried out by Pugwash in a project entitled 'A Nuclear-Weapon-Free World: Is It Desirable? Is It Feasible?'[9] The conclusion was that such a world is both desirable and feasible. It will not be easy, but it can be done.

It will take time to achieve it, perhaps 20–30 years. Time is needed firstly to put into operation the technological elements of the necessary safeguard system, such as dismantling all warheads under international control, disposing of the sensitive materials (highly-enriched uranium and plutonium), and instituting much more stringent supervision of the various processes involved in the peaceful utilization of nuclear energy. Time will also be needed to introduce certain political and societal changes, some of which contain an element of public education.

One of the political innovations is the acceptance of the universal validity of the treaty to abolish nuclear weapons. Once a certain number of states – including the present nuclear states – have agreed to the treaty, a resolution of the Security Council will make it binding on all states without exception. The treaty will make the possession of nuclear weapons a criminal offence; any transgression of it would be punishable, under international law, by the United Nations. The Gulf War was an illustration of the effectiveness of the international community in dealing with a transgression, when there is a general feeling that the cause justifies such action; surely, the illegal acquisition of nuclear weapons would be such a cause.

However, the main emphasis in the safeguard system of the treaty will be on preventing, rather than punishing, violations, and on the early detection of preparations to make nuclear weapons. In the first instance, this will require more openness, doing away with secrecy. All the nuclear research establishments will have either to close down or convert to peaceful research conducted openly. Openness is a *sine qua non* in science: secret research is a breach of a tenet of science. There will have to be much greater transparency in all societal activities.

Another feature of the treaty to eliminate nuclear weapons will be a clause that mandates all states to pass national laws making it the right and duty of every citizen to notify an international authority of any suspected attempt to violate the treaty. This will make every citizen, each of us, the custodian of the treaty. We call this system societal verification.[10] There will be a special role in it for the scientific community, to monitor the activities of scientists and the purchase of specialized equipment for making nuclear weapons. Whistle-blowing will be encouraged and immunity will have to be assured for the whistle-blowers. We believe that with these two verification systems, technological and societal, the probability of undetected break-out will be negligible.

A Nuclear-Weapon-Free World is a Safer World

All the same, no system can be made absolutely foolproof. There can be no 100 per cent guarantee that no break-out will occur, but the likelihood of such an occurrence will be much less than at present, when there is an abundance of nuclear weapons.

Who is likely to violate the treaty? Not a state governed by rational leaders, because they will realize that any advantage gained from the acquisition of a few bombs would be transient, and very costly in view of the severe retribution from the family of nations. This argument does not apply to a fanatical leader or to a group of terrorists, but the danger they pose is serious now. Should a terrorist group acquire an atom bomb, place it somewhere in a city and then demand a ransom, all the thousands of nuclear warheads in the arsenals of the world will be powerless against the threat. However, the likelihood of such a threat is much more likely now, when there are so many nuclear weapons and a growing black market in their constituents, than in a world in which there are no nuclear weapons.

Thus, while we cannot claim that a nuclear-weapon-free world would be absolutely safe against a nuclear threat, it would be safer than the present world, and much safer than the world of 20–30 years hence if the nuclear powers refuse to take definite steps towards the elimination of these weapons. This is so because the long-term alternative to a NWFW is not the present world, but one where a large number of other states have accepted the argument – now used by the nuclear states – that a nation which feels threatened in any way is entitled to its own nuclear deterrent. As Robert McNamara stated recently:[5]

> If we dare break out of the mindset that has guided the nuclear strategy of the nuclear powers for over four decades, I believe we can indeed 'put the genie back in the bottle'. If we do not, there is a substantial risk that the 21st century will witness a nuclear holocaust.

The lesson from 50 years of the nuclear age is that nuclear weapons are not needed for world security; indeed, they are a menace to world peace. A nuclear-weapon-free world is both desirable and feasible; only political will is needed to make it a reality.

References

1. *Statement on the Defence Estimates 1994*. Cmnd 2550. London: HMSO, 1994.
2. *Nuclear Posture Review*. US Department of Defense, September 1994.
3. *The Times*, 6 January 1989.
4. Holloway D. *Stalin and the Bomb*. Yale University Press, 1994.
5. McNamara RS. A long-range policy for nuclear forces of the nuclear powers. *Pugwash Newsletter* (Oct. 1994/Jan. 1995); **32**: 138.
6. Rifkind M. 'UK Defence Strategy: A Continuing Role for Nuclear Weapons?' Speech delivered at the Centre for Defence Studies, King's College, London, 16 November 1993.
7. Horner CA. Air force general calls for end to atomic arms. *Boston Globe*, 16 July 1994: 3.
8. Laird M. *The Washington Post*, 12 April 1992.
9. Rotblat J, Steinberger J, Udgaonkar B (eds). *A Nuclear-Weapon-Free World: Desirable? Feasible?* Oxford: Westview, 1993.
10. Rotblat J. Societal Verification. *Security Dialogue* 1992; **23**: 51.

(11 May 1995)

Joseph Rotblat is Emeritus Professor of Physics in the University of London at St Bartholomew's Hospital Medical College. During the Second World War he worked on the atomic bomb in Liverpool and Los Alamos but left when it became clear that Germany was not pursuing the bomb project. He has written extensively on the need for nuclear disarmament, and is President of the Pugwash Conferences on Science and World Affairs. He has recently become a fellow of the Royal Society.

Correspondence: Flat A, 63A Great Russell Street, London WC1B 3BJ.

Afterword

'... a new type of thinking is essential if mankind is to survive ...'
Albert Einstein[1]

The case for a nuclear-weapon-free world has, then, surely been made. What more is there to say?

This is being written immediately after the conclusion of the May 1995 Review Conference of the Non-Proliferation Treaty. In achieving an indefinite renewal of the treaty, the nuclear weapon states made it very clear that they did not want nuclear capability to spread to other countries, but also implicitly that their willingness to give up their own nuclear weapons was certainly not this year or next year but a remote 'sometime' which could all too easily be never. A 'Set of Principles' were adopted at the Review Conference which incorporate several points advocated by the contributors to this book. These include universal adherence to the treaty, in other words to join India, Israel and Pakistan, and full realization and effective implementation of Article VI. This entails a Comprehensive Test Ban Treaty by 1996, with utmost restraint by the nuclear-weapon-states until its entry into force (flouted by China within days and now apparently also by France); a ban on production of fissile material (but not mentioning tritium); and the 'ultimate' goal of eliminating nuclear weapons. No timetable was agreed for this programme, and the Principles are not legally binding on the nuclear weapon states. The UK government apparently does not intend to include Trident in negotiations for reductions until the US and Russian stockpiles are reduced to 'hundreds'.

The review process has been strengthened. Five-yearly review conferences will continue, with Preparatory Committees in each of the three years preceding the reviews, for example in 1997–8–9 before a Review Conference in 2000. The remit of these is 'to promote the full implementation of the Treaty, as well as its universality'. We can only hope that the ongoing review process set up by the conference will maintain sufficient pressure on the nuclear-weapon-states to keep their undertakings under Article VI of the treaty.

The commitment to a Comprehensive Test Ban Treaty is welcome, but, as Frank Barnaby showed earlier in this volume, the general principles governing fission bombs are well known, and the established nuclear powers know quite enough about fusion weapons not to need to test them; calls for 'safety' tests are in large part to ensure continued employment for the staff of the nuclear weapon laboratories against a day when new weapons might be called for. A declaration by the International Court of Justice that both use and threat of nuclear weapons is illegal would be helpful, but would all military men be as scrupulous as Commander Green believes the Royal Navy to be if the judgement of the Court implied that nuclear weapons should be taken off alert altogether?

Most of those working to free the world of nuclear weapons must have been told at some time that 'they can't be disinvented'. True, but nor can they be made overnight – and here the link with the civil nuclear industry is vital. All reactors produce plutonium, and by adjusting the burn-up period to a less than economic level the plutonium can be of an isotopic composition suitable for bomb-making. This calls in question the use of civil nuclear power but does not imply greater use of fossil fuels with their undesirable environmental effects. A variety of non-nuclear renewable energy sources are available,[2,3] and work on them would provide long-term employment for physicists and engineers.

This is only one aspect of sustainability. The bombings of Hiroshima and Nagasaki marked the end of the Second World War, but the intervening fifty years have not been an age of peace. More than 23 million people have died in some 150 conflicts around the world in this time.[4] Disputes over resources are a cause of war; the real reason for the massive Western reaction to the invasion of Kuwait by Iraq was oil, not human rights. Professor Rogers has explored these issues in depth elsewhere;[5,6] he fears that it will take the next fifty years to bring about a stable demilitarized society. Other authors have considered the environmental factors underlying political stability.[7]

The Commission on Global Governance examines pathways to a stable society. It calls for radical demilitarization including a nuclear-weapon-free world; democratization of the world economic system; reform of the United Nations, with abolition of the right of veto in the Security Council (significantly the Permanent Five with the veto are also the declared nuclear weapon states); and strengthening of international law with a greater role for the International Court of Justice.[8] The Commission stresses the values needed to underpin their proposals including respect for life, liberty, justice and equity, mutual respect and integrity.

This could be the new type of thinking that Einstein wanted. The ideas may not, in fact, be so new; similar precepts can be found in the sayings of the Buddha, in the Tao, in the Sermon on the Mount. The Commission on Global Governance has dressed them in late twentieth-century garb for the global village. They could not have been more obviously breached than by the bombings of Hiroshima and Nagasaki. We owe it to our children and succeeding generations to establish a society where another Hiroshima or Nagasaki is inconceivable.

(15 June 1995)   DOUGLAS HOLDSTOCK

References

1. Einstein A. Quoted in: Clark RW. *Einstein: The Life and Times*. London: Hodder and Stoughton 1973: 555.
2. Hutchinson GW. How should we get our energy? *Medicine and War* 1993; **9**: 4–18.
3. Flavin C. Harnessing the sun and the wind. In: Brown LR *et al. State of the World 1995*. London: Earthscan, 1995: 58–75.
4. Sivard RL. *World Military and Social Expenditures 1993*. Washington DC: World Priorities, 1993: 21.
5. Rogers P, Dando M. *A Violent Peace: Global Security After the Cold War*. London: Brassey's, 1992.
6. Rogers P. Renewing the quest for disarmament. Arms control North and South. In Childers E (ed). *Challenges to the United Nations: Building a Safer World*. London: Catholic Institute for International Relations/St Martin's Press, 1994: 135–151.
7. Myers N. *Ultimate Security: The Environmental Basis of Political Stability*. New York & London: WW Norton, 1993.
8. Commission on Global Governance. *Our Global Neighbourhood*. Oxford: Oxford University Press, 1995.

The Global Nuclear Arsenals – Beginning of 1995

FRANK BARNABY

The United States

As of early 1995, the American strategic nuclear arsenal consisted of 1,134 delivery systems (missiles and bombers), capable of delivering about 7,770 strategic nuclear warheads with a total explosive power of more than 2,000 megatons (equivalent to about 160,000 Hiroshima bombs).

The delivery systems include: 580 intercontinental ballistic missiles (ICBMs); 360 submarine-launched ballistic missiles (SLBMs); and 194 strategic bombers.

The ICBMs include 530 Minuteman IIIs and 50 MXs.

The SLBMs include 192 Trident I C-4s and 168 Trident II D-5s.

The strategic bombers include 95 B-1B Lancers, 5 B-2 Spirits and 94 B-52H Stratofortresses.

Of the ICBMs, each of 230 Minuteman IIIs is equipped with 3 Mark-12 multiple independently-targetable re-entry vehicles (MIRVs). These are W62 warheads, each with an explosive power of 170 kilotons. Each of the other 300 Minuteman III ICBMs is equipped with a Mark-12A MIRV carrying three W78 warheads, with an explosive power of 335 kilotons. Each MX ICBM carries 10 MIRVs. These are W87 warheads, each with an explosive power of 300 kilotons.

The 580 American ICBMs carry a total of 2,090 nuclear warheads which can deliver a total explosive power of about 570 megatons.

Each SLBM carries 8 MIRVs. Each Trident I C-4 SLBM carries W76 warheads with an explosive power of 100 kilotons. 118 of the Trident II D-5 SLBMs also carry W76 warheads; the other 50 carry W88 warheads, each with an explosive power of 475 kilotons. The American Navy is operating a fleet of 15 strategic nuclear submarines.

The 360 American SLBMs carry a total of 2,880 warheads which can deliver a total explosive power of about 440 megatons.

The Lancer and Spirit strategic bombers carry B53, B61, and B83 bombs; the Stratofortresses carry these bombs, air-launched cruise missiles and advanced cruise missiles. The bomber force carries a total of 1,000 air-launched cruise missiles, 400 advanced cruise missiles, and 1,400 bombs.

The 194 strategic bombers carry a total of 2,800 nuclear warheads having a total explosive power of about 1,200 megatons.

After the START II Treaty has been implemented, by the year 2003, the United States operational strategic nuclear arsenal will include at most:

> 500 Minuteman III ICBMs, each carrying a single W87 warhead; 336 Trident II SLBMs on 14 Ohio-Class strategic nuclear submarines, carrying a total of 1,680 (1,280 W76 and 400 W88) warheads; and 84 strategic bombers (20 B-2As and 64 B-52Hs) carrying about 950 bombs and 400 advanced cruise missiles.

These forces will carry a total of about 3,500 operational strategic nuclear warheads. It is realistic to assume that the Americans will retain about the same number of strategic nuclear warheads in reserve. They plan to deploy about 1,000 tactical nuclear weapons (sea-launched cruise missiles and tactical bombs). In the year 2003, therefore, the American nuclear arsenal may include about 8,500 warheads – 3,500 in active strategic service, 3,500 in reserve, and 1,000 tactical nuclear weapons.

In 1990, for comparison, the American nuclear stockpile included a total of about 20,500 nuclear warheads. By the year 2003, a total of about 12,000 warheads may be removed from the arsenal for dismantlement.

Russia

As of early 1995, the Russian (CIS) strategic nuclear arsenal consisted of 1,452 delivery systems (missiles and bombers), capable of delivering about 8,500 strategic nuclear warheads with a total explosive power of more than 3,600 megatons (equivalent to about 300,000 Hiroshima bombs).

The delivery systems include: 887 ICBMs; 456 SLBMs; and about 100 strategic bombers.

The ICBMs include 248 SS-18s, 260 SS-19, 46 SS-24, and 333 SS-25s.

The SLBMs include 224 SS-N-18s, 120 SS-N-20, and 112 SS-N-23.

The bombers include 84 Tu-95 Bears and 25 Tu-160 Blackjacks.

Of the ICBMs, each of SS-18s is equipped with 10 MIRVs; each SS-19 with 6 MIRVs; each SS-24 with 10 MIRVs; and each SS-25 carries a single warhead. The ICBM warheads generally have an explosive power of about 550 kilotons.

The 887 Russian (CIS) ICBMs carry a total of 4,833 nuclear warheads which can deliver a total explosive power of about 2,700 megatons.

Of the SLBMs, each SS-N-18 carries 3 MIRVs (explosive power 500 kilotons); each SS-N-20 carries 10 MIRVs (explosive power 200 kilotons); and each SS-N-23 carries 4 MIRVs (explosive power 100 kilotons).

The Russian Navy is operating a fleet of 27 strategic nuclear submarines.

The 456 Russian SLBMs carry a total of 2,320 warheads which can deliver a total explosive power of about 620 megatons.

Russian (CIS) strategic bombers carry bombs, short-range attack missiles and air-launched cruise missiles. A total of about 1,300 missiles and bombs are carried with a total explosive power of about 340 megatons.

After the START II Treaty has been implemented, by the year 2003, the Russian operational strategic nuclear arsenal will probably include about:

800 ICBMs (SS-19s and SS-25s), each carrying a single warhead;

400 SLBMs on about 24 strategic nuclear submarines, carrying a total of about 1,700 warheads; and 75 Bear and Blackjack strategic bombers carrying about 1,000 bombs and cruise missiles.

These forces will carry a total of about 3,500 operational strategic nuclear warheads. The number of tactical nuclear weapons which the Russians intend to retain on active service is not known is not known. The announced figures vary from zero to about 2,000. In comparison, in 1990, for example, the Russian (CIS) nuclear stockpile included a total of about 38,000 nuclear warheads. By the year 2003, a total of more than 30,000 warheads may be removed from the arsenal for dismantlement.

The United Kingdom

The British strategic nuclear force is carried in Polaris strategic nuclear submarines. Of the four Polaris ballistic-missile submarines, the first was decommissioned in May 1992 as part of the programme to replace them by four Trident submarines around the year 2000. The first British Trident completed sea trials in January 1993 and entered operational service in early 1995.

Each Trident submarine can carry 16 Trident D-5 SLBMs. The eight warheads on each SLBM are MIRVed. Each Polaris missile carries three warheads but they are not independently targetable. The Trident missiles have much greater ranges (12,000 kilometres compared to Polaris's 4,630 kilometres) and are much more accurate.

The United Kingdom government has announced that it will not deploy more than 96 Trident D-5 SLBM warheads on each Trident submarine, instead of the 128 on each of the Polaris submarines. (Under the START II Treaty, US Trident II SLBMs can carry only 4 warheads each, and the United Kingdom will be under international pressure to follow suit.)

The UK government has announced the cancellation of its participation in an Anglo-French development of a tactical air-to-surface missile to replace the WE-177 free-fall nuclear aircraft bombs by the year 2005. Trident will now be used in a tactical as well as a strategic role, eventually becoming the UK's only nuclear weapon system.

The number of WE-177 A/B gravity bombs has been reduced by a half, to about 80. All (about 25) the WE-177C nuclear strike/depth bombs carried on Royal Naval helicopters have been taken out of service and dismantled.

Other British tactical nuclear weapons – Lance surface-to-surface missiles and nuclear artillery shells – have been phased out.

France

France currently deploys about 500 nuclear warheads. Of these, 384 are carried on SLBMs; 18 are on land-based intermediate-range land-based ballistic missiles (IRBMs); and about 80 on air-to-surface missiles on aircraft. In May 1992 France announced that it would reduce the number of new strategic nuclear submarines it plans to build from six to four.

The first of these Le Triomphant-class submarines is scheduled to go into service in March 1996. The second is under construction. All four are expected to enter service by the year 2005. These submarines will replace the five strategic nuclear submarines now in service.

The new submarines will carry the M-45 SLBMs, expected to carry 6 MIRVs each. In about 2005, the M-5 SLBM, each carrying up to 8 MIRVs, now under development, will become operational. This forecast may, however, be over optimistic.

France also deploys 18 SSBS S-3D IRBMs, each carrying a single warhead. There are 45 Mirage 2000 N aircraft, each equipped with an air-to-surface nuclear missiles. Another 15 Mirage IV P aircraft, also equipped with air-to-surface missiles, will remain in service until 1996 when their task will be taken over by new Rafale aircraft. The French Navy operates 24 Super Etendard carrier-based aircraft, each carrying an air-to-surface nuclear missile.

China

China continues to modernize and increase its nuclear forces. It appears that the Chinese are developing two new solid-fuel mobile ICBMs, including a MIRVed system which could be used as an SLBM. China probably deploys about 14 ICBMs – 4 CSS-4s and about 10 CSS-3s, each carrying a single warhead with an explosive power of about 1,000 kilotons. In addition, there are about 60 CSS-2 IRBMs each carrying a similar warhead.

The Chinese Navy deploys one Xia-Class strategic nuclear submarine carrying 12 CSS-N-3 SLBMs, each carrying a nuclear warhead, probably with an explosive power of about 300 kilotons. A new SLBM, the CSS-N-4 is under development, probably for deployment in the late 1990s. This is a variant of the new ICBM under development, with a range of about 8,000 kilometres and which will probably carry a warhead with an explosive power of about 300 kilotons.

The Chinese may be operating about 150 aircraft – each probably carrying a nuclear bomb. Of these, about 120 are H-6 bombers, with a range of about 3,000 kilometres.

(15 May 1995)

Index